P-40 WARHAWK
VS
Ki-43 OSCAR
China 1944–45

CARL MOLESWORTH

First published in Great Britain in 2008 by Osprey Publishing,
Midland House, West Way, Botley, Oxford OX2 0PH, UK
443 Park Avenue South, New York, NY 10016, USA

E-mail: info@ospreypublishing.com

A CIP catalog record for this book is available from the British Library

ISBN: 978 1 84603 295 0

Edited by Tony Holmes
Cover artwork, three-views and cockpit and armament scrap views by Jim Laurier
Battlescene by Jim Laurier
Index by Alan Thatcher
Typeset in Adobe Garamond and ITC Conduit
Originated by PDQ Digital Media Solutions
Printed in China through Worldprint

08 09 10 11 12   10 9 8 7 6 5 4 3 2 1

For a catalog of all books published by Osprey Military and Aviation please contact:

NORTH AMERICA
Osprey Direct, c/o Random House Distribution Center, 400 Hahn Road,
Westminster, MD 21157

E-mail: info@ospreydirect.com

ALL OTHER REGIONS
Osprey Direct UK, PO Box 140 Wellingborough, Northants, NN8 2FA, UK

E-mail: info@ospreydirect.co.uk

www.ospreypublishing.com

Osprey Publishing is supporting the Woodland Trust, the UK's leading woodland
conservation charity, by funding the dedication of trees.

Acknowledgments

The book that you are about to read has been a team
effort from start to finish. In 30 years of researching air
combat during World War II, I have concentrated almost
entirely on USAAF fighter units involved in the conflict.
The veterans of the Fourteenth Air Force, and their family
members, who have contributed material to my previous
books also made this volume possible.

This is my first attempt to tell both sides of a combat,
so I had to call on several people to help me fill out the
Japanese elements of the story. Hiroshi Ichimura not only
provided details culled from his own research about the
JAAF's Ki-43 units that fought in China, but he also
made photographs available from the extensive collection
of Yasuho Izawa that are a vital element in this book. I am
most deeply indebted to both men for their important
contributions. Finally, I would like to thank aviation artist
Jim Laurier for his work on this volume, which, as always,
is magnificent.

P-40 cover art

After a six-week siege, the Chinese city of Hengyang fell
to the Japanese on August 8, 1944. That morning, eight
P-40s of the 75th Fighter Squadron (FS), led by Maj
Donald Quigley, encountered nine Ki-43s of the 48th
Sentai at low altitude near Hengshan during a strafing
mission. Following a brief action, the 75th FS returned
to base and claimed one victory, two probables and four
damaged. However, the 48th Sentai had actually lost
three Ki-43s, while the sentai commander, Maj Masao
Matsuo, was wounded. No P-40s were lost, although the
48th Sentai pilots claimed seven victories.
(Artwork by Jim Laurier)

Ki-43 cover art

Another encounter between Ki-43s and P-40s occurred
during the afternoon of August 8, 1944 when 16 'Oscars'
of the 25th Sentai and 11 Warhawks of the 3rd Fighter
Group (FG)/Chinese-American Composite Wing
(CACW) clashed near Sinshih. Led by Lt Col William N
Reed, the P-40s had been strafing river traffic on the
Yangtze when the Ki-43s attacked from above and behind.
The fight evolved into a swirling dogfight at low altitude,
and one Ki-43 was shot down (pilot survived) and four
P-40s were damaged. The CACW pilots claimed nine
victories upon their return to base.
(Artwork by Jim Laurier)

CONTENTS

INTRODUCTION

In the annals of aerial warfare, no aircraft type has come to symbolize a campaign in which it fought as did the Curtiss P-40 Warhawk in China in 1941–45. Known the world over for the distinctive sharksmouth warpaint on their noses, P-40 fighters first saw combat in China with the legendary American Volunteer Group (AVG), and continued to fight while equipping squadrons of the US Army Air Forces (USAAF) throughout World War II.

Just as ubiquitous as the P-40 in the skies over China during World War II was its most common Japanese Army Air Force (JAAF) adversary, the Nakajima Ki-43, or Type 1 Hayabusa, codenamed "Oscar" by the Allies. Though never achieving the iconic status of the P-40, the Ki-43 nevertheless proved a worthy opponent whenever the aircraft met in combat.

These two aircraft types were the products of vastly different, yet contemporary, philosophies of fighter design. The P-40 reflected the thinking of American war planners in the late 1930s. It was heavily armed, sturdy and reasonably fast at medium and low altitudes, with armor plate protection for the pilot and self-sealing fuel tanks. Its inline Allison engine was powerful and reliable. The price paid by the P-40 for these attributes was weight, which contributed to its slow rate-of-climb and sluggish performance at high altitude.

The Ki-43 was a stiletto to the battle-ax P-40. A logical extension of World War I fighter thinking and the Samurai tradition combined in one airframe, the Ki-43 design favored maneuverability over all other characteristics. Light weight and a large wing area gave it a small turning radius and a high rate-of-climb – just what a pilot needed for close-in dogfighting. But to achieve the Ki-43's low wing loading, its designers had to sacrifice firepower (the aeroplane only carried two machine guns) and survivability.

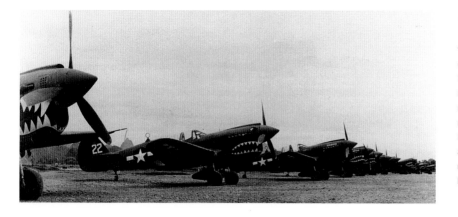

Although the P-40 and Ki-43 met in combat throughout the Pacific war from New Guinea and the Solomon Islands to the steaming jungles of Burma, their duel peaked during the air campaign that accompanied the Japanese *Ichi-Go* land offensive in China during 1944. The classic engagements over the Hsiang River Valley during the siege of Hengyang are the focus of this book.

Day after day during the summer of 1944, P-40s and Ki-43s clashed in the skies over China. Although the Chinese and American pilots under the command of MajGen Claire L. Chennault maintained air superiority, the Japanese ground offensive ultimately achieved its goals of capturing Allied air bases in East China and completing a land link from French Indo-China to the great port city of Shanghai.

There was a very human story to the aerial clashes in *Ichi-Go*, with fighter pilots on both sides displaying courage, imagination and flying skill in great measure. Sadly, the personal accounts of this campaign that survive are largely limited to those of the P-40 pilots. Much to the author's frustration, few if any personal stories by or about Ki-43 pilots who flew in China have come to light – and certainly none in the English language. There are several reasons for this.

Firstly, it is important to understand how few Japanese fighter pilots were involved in the China campaign. The JAAF had just two Ki-43 sentais, with an authorized strength of 57 pilots each, and considerably fewer pilots and aircraft actually available for operations at any given time. Combat inevitably took its toll on both men and machines, and the JAAF was not able to provide replacements in sufficient numbers to maintain the units at full strength.

The fact that Japan ultimately lost the war also helps to explain the dearth of personal accounts. The nation's Bushido code of warrior values, which stressed death before dishonor, caused many pilots who survived the conflict to suffer deep feelings of personal shame. They were neither inclined nor encouraged to record their stories post-war, and many records of the units in which they served were destroyed as the conflict drew to a close. So, as the succeeding years have passed, these pilots died in silence, and their stories of air combat in China went with them to their graves.

It may strike the readers of this book as ironic that we know more about the technical aspects of the Ki-43 as a weapon of war than we know about the men who risked their lives to fly it in combat. That is a fair assessment, and a sad one at that.

CHRONOLOGY

1931

Sept 18 Japan invades Manchuria. Conquest complete by January 1932.

1937

May 31 Capt Claire L. Chennault arrives in China to serve as an advisor to the Chinese Air Force (CAF).

June 6 US Army Air Corps (USAAC) issues a contract for production of the Curtiss P-36 monoplane fighter.

July 7 Chinese and Japanese ground forces clash at Marco Polo Bridge, west of Peking, setting off Japan's invasion of China.

December Nakajima Ki-27 Type 97 (the JAAF's first modern monoplane fighter) is ordered into production, and development contract for the next generation fighter, to become the Ki-43 Type 1 Hayabusa, granted to Nakajima.

This Curtiss 81-A2 started its combat career as aircraft "19"/CAF serial P-8146 with the 1st PS AVG. When the latter was disbanded on July 4, 1942, the airplane was turned over to the 23rd FG, where it was assigned to the 74th FS at Kunming. Note the heavily weathered and repainted camouflage, and the tricolor pinwheel design on the hubcaps. (Leon Klesman)

1938

October Japanese forces capture Hankow and Canton, and Chinese resistance shifts to guerrilla operations.

Oct 14 First flight of the Curtiss XP-40 (a modified P-36 airframe).

1939

January First flight of the Ki-43 prototype.

April 26 USAAC orders P-40 into production.

1941

July 4 AVG is formed with 100 Curtiss H-81 (export P-40) fighters and American personnel, commanded by Chennault, to protect the Burma Road supply line from Rangoon, in Burma, to China.

October Deliveries of the first production Ki-43s to the JAAF.

Dec 7 Japan attacks American military targets at Pearl Harbor, Hawaii, causing the United States to declare war against Japan and Germany.

Dec 25 Ki-43 and P-40 meet in combat for the first time over Rangoon.

Air combat in China was a serious business, as can be seen on the face of Lt Tadahiko Toki of the 1st Chutai/25th Sentai as he sits in the cockpit of his Ki-43-I. Toki was killed in action during an air battle with P-40s of the 75th FS/23rd FG on April 1, 1943 over Lingling. (Yasuho Izawa)

1942
July 4   USAAF's China Air Task Force (CATF) replaces AVG at Kunming, in China.

1943
March   USAAF's Fourteenth Air Force replaces CATF in China.

1944
April 17   Japan begins *Ichi-Go* advance in China.
June 16   Fourteenth Air Force abandons its forward airbase at Hengyang, and P-40 squadrons retreat to Kweilin and Liuchow.
August 8   Chinese forces at Hengyang surrender after 44-day siege.
Nov 24   Japanese capture Nanning, completing the *Ichi-Go* objective to establish a rail link from French Indo-China to Hankow, Shanghai and Peking.

1945
March   25th Sentai completes conversion from Ki-43 to Ki-84.
May   Chinese forces stop the *Ichi-Go* offensive short of Chihkiang.
June   27th FS/5th FG CACW becomes the last squadron in the Fourteenth Air Force to convert from P-40s to P-51s.

MajGen Claire L. Chennault (left), commander of the Fourteenth Air Force, plots strategy with Col Clinton D. "Casey" Vincent, commander of the 68th CW, during the Japanese *Ichi-Go* offensive of 1944. The P-40 squadrons of the 68th clashed repeatedly with Ki-43s of the 5th Air Army during the campaign. (David Brown)

DESIGN AND DEVELOPMENT

P-40 WARHAWK

The Curtiss P-40 series had such a long and involved development history that it is difficult to say when the process actually began. Do the roots of the P-40 spring from the various Curtiss Hawk biplane fighters produced in the 1920s and early 1930s? Or does the story start with the XP-934 Swift of 1932, which was the unsuccessful first attempt by Curtiss to build a monoplane fighter? Perhaps the former, perhaps the latter, or perhaps a little of both. But the fact remains that by the early 1930s, those designs, and others, had helped to establish the Curtiss Aeroplane Division of the Curtiss-Wright Corporation as one of the leading manufacturers of military aircraft in the United States, if not the world.

In 1934, Curtiss initiated the design of a new monoplane fighter, the Hawk 75. The design team, led by former Northrop engineer Donovan H. Berlin, was instructed to come up with a fighter that could win a USAAC contract competition the following year. Berlin's team created a low-wing monoplane that featured a fully enclosed cockpit and retractable landing gear, and was powered by a 900hp Wright twin-row radial engine.

The airplane first flew in April 1935, but failed to win the Army contract, which went to the Seversky P-35. Instead, the Army ordered three Curtiss service test aircraft and designated them Y1P-36s. USAAC officials were greatly impressed by the improvements the company had made with this machine when compared with the original H-75, and in June 1937 they issued Curtiss with a contract to build 210 P-36s. France quickly followed with an additional order for 200 fighters.

By all accounts the P-36 was an excellent aircraft, with a robust airframe, reliable powerplant and lively flying characteristics. In fact, the Royal Air Force flew export versions of the airplane against the Japanese in Burma well into 1944. But as early as 1938, it became obvious that the 300mph top speed of the P-36 was not fast enough to allow the aircraft to remain competitive with the advanced fighter designs emerging from Europe.

Donovan Berlin went back to work on the H-75 design, replacing the radial engine with a turbo-supercharged version of the new Allison V-1710 liquid-cooled inline powerplant and moving the cockpit aft to offset the additional weight in the nose. The streamlined XP-37 delivered a performance boost as expected, achieving a top speed of 340mph in initial testing. The Army ordered 13 service test models of the YP-37, but the experimental turbo-supercharger proved unreliable and sightlines from the cockpit were very poor, so further development of the airplane was abandoned. The seed of an idea had been planted, however, a seed that soon would bloom in the form of the legendary Curtiss P-40.

Berlin returned to the basic P-36 design again for his next attempt to build a high-performance fighter, but this time he took a simpler path. Recognizing that the USAAC believed it needed a fighter that produced maximum performance at an altitude of just 15,000ft, Donovan did away with the complex turbo-supercharging system of the P-37 and simply mated a 1,050hp Allison V-1710-19 engine, with conventional supercharging, to the airframe of the tenth production P-36A. The new

The Curtiss P-36, designed in 1934 as the Hawk 75, was the predecessor to the P-40. The groundcrew seen here, possibly at Selfridge Field, are attempting to start the engine by pulling on the propeller with a sling-and-cable device. The first P-40 was actually a production P-36A fitted with an Allison V12 liquid-cooled engine. (Ed Bollen)

fighter, already designated the XP-40 by the USAAC, had a long, pointed nose similar to the P-37's and the radiator mounted under the fuselage aft of the trailing edge of the wing.

The XP-40 made its maiden flight on October 14, 1938, with Curtiss assistant chief test pilot Ed Elliott at the controls. The airplane looked fast, but in initial testing it was unable to top 340mph at 15,000ft. Various tweaks to the design followed, including moving the radiator into a cowling under the nose and replacing the engine with a more powerful V-1710-33, but its speed remained disappointing.

The P-40 had other strengths, however. Its handling was generally good, although the airplane wasn't as maneuverable as the P-36, and it had spectacular diving speed. But, most importantly, it was available. Converting the Curtiss factory from production of the P-36 to the similar P-40 would be a relatively simple task, compared to gearing up to build an entirely new aircraft.

By January 1939, when the USAAC held its next fighter competition, tensions were already rising in Europe and the Far East. Although isolationist sentiment remained high in the United States, Congress had appropriated funds for a major build-up of the nation's military forces, including the acquisition of a large number of new fighter aircraft. After comparing the XP-40 to other fighter proposals that were not yet as far along in development, such as the Lockheed P-38 and the Bell P-39, the USAAC issued a record-setting contract to Curtiss on April 26, 1939 for 524 P-40s at a cost of nearly $13 million.

Although the XP-40 had yet to satisfy the desired performance specifications set out by the USAAC, the low price and quick availability of the new Curtiss fighter had carried the day. More advanced designs – especially the P-38 – promised speed and altitude performance far superior to the P-40, but their manufacturers would require at least two years before they could begin delivering them to the Army. Deliveries of the P-40 could start in half that time, allowing the USAAC to embark on its build-up while Lockheed and other manufacturers developed the next generation of American fighters.

The Army chose to skip the option of ordering Y-prefixed service test aircraft and went directly to the P-40 production model. Designated the Hawk 81 by Curtiss, the production model featured the "Dash-33" Allison engine and carried four machine guns – two 0.50-in. weapons in the upper cowling and one 0.30-in. in each wing. Meanwhile, the Curtiss engineers continued to massage the design in the quest for more speed. In December 1939, the modified XP-40 reached 366mph at the desired altitude, satisfying the Army that the P-40 was sufficiently developed to go into mass production.

The first production P-40 (serial number 39-156) rolled off the Curtiss production line in March 1940. The airplane, along with the next two off the line, went through a series of tests that determined its top speed was 357mph at 15,000ft, its cruising speed was 277mph and its landing speed was 80mph. The P-40's service ceiling was 32,750ft, and it could climb 3,080ft during the first minute of flight, reaching 15,000ft in 5.3 minutes. Deliveries of the first 200 P-40s to the USAAC began in June 1940. In time, the P-40 would acquire the name "Warhawk" in Army service.

P-40N-5 WARHAWK

33ft 5.75in.

12ft 4.5in.

37ft 3.5in.

Curtiss also began producing an export version of the Hawk 81, which was dubbed the Tomahawk. France had been the first country to place an order, but none of the 185 H-81-A1s it purchased in May 1939 had been delivered prior to the nation being occupied by German forces just over a year later. Great Britain was by then desperate to obtain additional fighters for the RAF so it took over the French aircraft, along with placing its own order for Tomahawks.

Sources disagree as to whether Curtiss produced a P-40A or not, but the first significant upgrade to the line was the P-40B, or H-81A-2. The changes in this model were the product of intelligence gleaned from the air battles that took place during the first year of the war in Europe. They included refinements such as self-sealing fuel tanks, armor protection for the pilot behind the seat and in the windscreen and the addition of one 0.30-in. machine gun in each wing. New self-sealing tanks were introduced in the P-40C, these reducing the internal fuel capacity from 160 gal down to 135 gal. The provision to carry an external 52 gal drop tank on the centerline was added to compensate. Each of these items added weight, and the performance of the new models – particularly their rate-of-climb – suffered accordingly. But these were the first models of the P-40 to be truly combat-capable.

The first P-40s to see action were actually RAF Tomahawks in North Africa in June 1941. The strengths and weaknesses of the Curtiss fighter soon made themselves apparent in combat against German and Italian adversaries. Commonwealth pilots quickly came to appreciate the Tomahawk as a stable gun platform with a reliable powerplant and a robust airframe, capable of absorbing battle damage sufficient to bring down most of its contemporaries.

The British replaced the 0.30-in. wing guns with their own 0.303-in. weapons to simplify supply problems, and pilots found this armament sufficient for desert warfare. The Tomahawk's maneuverability and dive speed also made the fighter competitive with the German Bf 109E/Fs and Italian C.202s it met in combat. The Tomahawk's major shortcoming for desert combat, however, was its poor performance at higher altitudes.

Top Australian ace Clive Caldwell, who scored 20.5 victories in Curtiss fighters, noted that while the Tomahawk performed creditably in a dogfight if operating within its own altitude limitations, pilots were forced to leave the initiative with their higher flying opponents. In order to engage the enemy at the Tomahawk's best height, pilots soon learned to accept the fact that they had to endure an initial attack from above.

Aviators from at least eight different nations flew P-40s and Tomahawks during the H-81's operational combat life. Perhaps the most famous of these airplanes were the 100 Tomahawks diverted from the British in 1941 to equip the AVG in Burma and China.

While the Curtiss factory worked around the clock turning out P-40s and Tomahawks, Allison engineers were busy developing a more powerful version of the V-1710 engine. The 1,150hp Allison F (V-1710-39) was initially slated for the new Curtiss XP-46 fighter, but the Army did not want to shut down the company's production plant long enough to convert to the new fighter. Curtiss, meanwhile, had redesigned the P-40 with the new engine to fill a British order in May 1940. The Army bought 22 examples of the new H-87A Kittyhawk as the P-40D in September 1940, and soon followed this initial purchase up with orders for 820 P-40Es.

The H-87A was a major departure from the earlier models, as it boasted a totally new fuselage. A change in gearing moved up the thrust line of the V-1710-39 engine, and thus the center of the propeller spinner, so that it was now nearly in line with the exhaust stacks. With the higher line of thrust, the fuselage was shortened by 6.75in., and the radiator/oil cooler chin scoop was deepened. The upper section of the fuselage was cut down, and a larger cockpit opening gave the pilot improved vision.

Armament also changed in the H-87A. The nose guns were removed, and two 0.50-in. weapons were installed in each wing, along with an improved system of hydraulic gun chargers. The nearly identical H-87A-3/P-40E featured six wing guns, with 281 rounds of ammunition per gun. A 500lb bomb or 52 gal drop tank could be fitted on the centerline shackle, and six 20lb bombs could be mounted to attachments on the undersides of the wings.

The improvements in the P-40D/E did not translate into significantly better speed or altitude performance over prior models, however. Top speed was 355mph at 15,000ft, and the service ceiling dropped to 29,000ft. Range was a respectable 800 miles at normal speeds and 1,150 miles at 195mph.

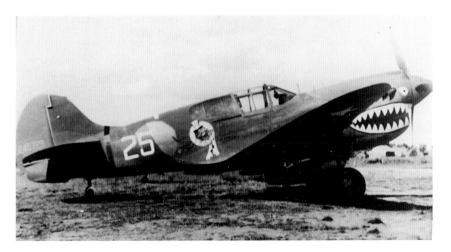

The Curtiss P-40K was the most numerous fighter in the Fourteenth Air Force from late 1942 until early 1944. Aircraft "25" (42-45723) was assigned to the 74th FS/23rd FG in 1943, and it displays the squadron's red band around the fuselage just forward of the tail. Also of note is the prominent 23rd FG "flying tiger" badge, and the two-tone painted-out national insignia on the fuselage. (Jim Crow via Dwayne Tabatt)

OPPOSITE
This Ki-43-II was regularly flown by ace WO Iwataro Hazawa of the 2nd Chutai/ 25th Sentai, based at Hankow, in China, during the summer of 1944. Its camouflage was uneven dark green (similar to Federal Standard 4094) over natural metal. The color of the tail stripe denoted the individual chutais within the 25th – white for the 1st, red for the 2nd and yellow for the 3rd.

When a supply of Rolls-Royce-designed Merlin engines became available in 1941, a P-40D was modified to accept the powerplant made famous in the RAF's Spitfire and Hurricane fighters. Designated the P-40F/Kittyhawk II, the new version had a slightly different nose that had a deeper chin inlet and lacked the air scoop on top of the cowling. Partway through its production run of 1,311, the P-40F got a 26-in. extension to the rear of the fuselage to improve directional stability. This feature carried over to the P-40L, which Curtiss attempted to lighten by deleting two wing guns and other equipment. The Merlin 28 engine, built in the US by Packard, featured a single-stage, two-speed supercharger that offered modestly better altitude performance than the Allison engine. Other than that, the performance of the P-40F/L was similar to earlier models.

The next Allison-powered H-87, the P-40K or Kittyhawk III, featured an improved V-1710-73 and an enlarged vertical tail, the latter being yet another attempt to improve directional stability. This aircraft also got the 26-in. fuselage extension late in its production run, and the similar P-40M that followed it also had this feature.

The last major version of the H-87, and the most numerous, was the P-40N/ Kittyhawk IV series. In the P-40N, powered by the same Allison V-1710-81 that equipped the P-40M, Curtiss engineers took the lightening efforts started in the P-40L several steps further, and in the process produced the fastest production model with a top speed of 378mph. But there was a price to pay for the slight increase in speed. The P-40N-1's armament was reduced to four guns and its front wing tank and internal starter were removed – none of these deletions were well received by frontline pilots using the N-model on combat operations.

Various improvements were introduced in the eight sub-variants of the P-40N that followed, the most visible of these being a modified cockpit canopy with a frameless sliding hood and the cut-down rear fuselage deck of the P-40N-5, which also reverted to six-gun armament.

The last Warhawk, P-40N-40 (serial number 44-47964) rolled out of the Curtiss factory on November 30, 1944, completing a production run of 13,738 aircraft.

Ki-43 OSCAR

Although the Nakajima Ki-43 was vastly different from the Curtiss P-40 in concept and design, the development paths of the two fighters were remarkably similar. Like Curtiss in the United States, Nakajima Hikoki KK was already an established Japanese manufacturer of military aircraft by the mid-1930s. Starting with the A1N1 naval carrier fighter – a license-built version of the Gloster Gambet – in 1925, Nakajima turned out a steady stream of successful fighters for the Japanese Naval Air Force (JNAF) and JAAF. Most of these in-house designs were biplanes, including the outstanding A2N carrier fighter of 1930, although Nakajima also produced the Type 91 parasol monoplane fighter for the Army.

When the JAAF sought proposals in 1935 for a new single-seat monoplane fighter, Nakajima, and its rivals Kawasaki and Mitsubishi, responded with three designs.

Ki-43-II OSCAR

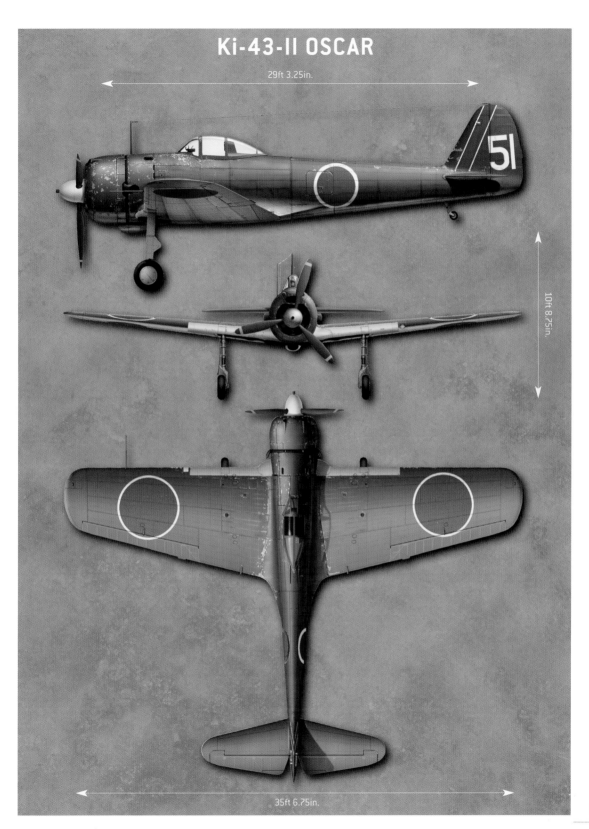

29ft 3.25in.

10ft 8.75in.

35ft 6.75in.

The Kawasaki Ki-28, Mitsubishi Ki-33 and Nakajima Ki-12 all promised a good turn of speed, but that was not to be the determining characteristic when the JAAF flight-tested the prototypes in early 1937. Army planners were also looking for maneuverability, light weight and simplicity in their new fighter, and that is what they found in Nakajima's Ki-27.

Conceived by Nakajima engineers Yasumi Koyama and Professor Hideo Itokawa, the Ki-27 embodied the smallest practical airframe that could be designed around the best available radial engine, Nakajima's Ha-1-Ko. This nine-cylinder powerplant produced 710hp for take-off and 650hp at 6,560ft. The airplane featured all-metal stressed-skin construction, with an oval-section semi-monocoque fuselage, a large wing employing an NN-2 airfoil section, a fixed undercarriage housed in streamlined fairings and a sliding canopy over the cockpit. The clean lines of the Ki-27 were in keeping with the old axiom that when an aircraft looks right, it usually flies well.

With a wing loading of 14.33lb per square foot, the Ki-27 was markedly more maneuverable than its rivals for the JAAF contract, while nearly matching them in maximum speed and rate-of-climb. An order for ten pre-production aircraft was issued, and at the end of service trials in December 1937, the Imperial Army placed a large-quantity order for the Ki-27-Ko, featuring a more powerful Ha-1-Otsu engine, a variable-pitch propeller and two 7.7mm machine guns.

Deliveries of the new fighter began in March 1938, and within weeks the Ki-27 had scored its first combat success when Capt Tateo Kato claimed the destruction of three Chinese-flown Polikarpov I-15 fighters over northern China. Understandably, Army pilots were ecstatic about their new mount. By this time, however, Nakajima engineers were already designing the fighter that would become its successor.

Politics were to play a major role in shaping the concept and design of Nakajima's next fighter. The company had been the only manufacturer to come away from the Army fighter competition of 1937 with an order for airplanes. That meant Kawasaki and Mitsubishi had been left to bear the tremendous costs that they had invested into their prototypes. To forestall the chance of this happening again, they began lobbying the Japanese Diet (government) for a change in procurement policy to eliminate the

Chinese and American groundcrew at Kweilin inspect a Nakajima Ki-27 captured in China during late 1942. The Ki-27 was the JAAF's first modern fighter, flying in frontline service from 1938 through 1942, before being replaced by another Nakajima product, the Ki-43. Both airplanes were noted for their outstanding maneuverability. (Jack Best)

competitive selection of military aircraft. The lawmakers agreed, and orders were passed to Army Air Headquarters that a single manufacturer would supply the next fighter.

With Nakajima being the only aircraft company that had proven its ability to produce a modern fighter to the Army's satisfaction, it was abundantly clear which manufacturer would get the contract for the Ki-27's replacement. Nakajima received the development contract for the Army's next generation fighter, the Ki-43, in December 1937.

The immediate combat success of the Ki-27 in China served to support the Army's philosophy of favoring light weight and maneuverability in its fighter aircraft. With the same generals in charge of procuring the Ki-43 and the same team of engineers designing the airplane, it is hardly a surprise that the new fighter would represent an uninspiring small step forward in aviation technology. The generals instructed Nakajima to produce a fighter that would have maneuverability at least equal to the Ki-27, but with greater speed, a faster rate-of-climb and longer range. And that is what Nakajima eventually gave them, but just barely.

Following the pattern set by the Ki-27, Koyama and Itokawa again set out to produce the smallest and lightest possible airplane around the best available radial engine, which was now the 14-cylinder Nakajima Ha-25. The Ki-43 was another aerodynamically clean low-wing, stressed-skin all-metal monoplane. Its three-spar, one-piece wing had metal-framed control surfaces covered in fabric and contained four fuel tanks with a total capacity of 125 gal. Again, two 7.7mm machine guns were mounted in the upper decking of the forward fuselage. The only major departure from the earlier design was the inclusion of hydraulically operated folding undercarriage members.

The first Ki-43 prototype was rolled out on December 12, 1938, and it was immediately disappointing. Not only was the airplane seven percent heavier than its calculated structural weight, but initial flight tests at Tachikawa revealed it lacked the responsiveness and maneuverability of the Ki-27. To make matters worse, the Ki-43 proved barely faster than the Ki-27, and its landing gear was difficult to retract and lower. Perhaps the only successful element of the Ki-43 was its Ha-25 engine, and that was a copy of an American design.

When the disappointed JAAF threatened to cancel further development of the Ki-43, Nakajima's designers went back to the drawing board. They refined and lightened the airframe, reducing the fuselage cross-section and redesigning the aft section and tail surfaces. An all-around-vision cockpit canopy was introduced as well.

Perhaps the most important change in the redesigned Ki-43 was the addition of the so-called "butterfly" combat flap. This Fowler-type flap could be deployed to increase lift, giving the airplane a dramatically tighter turning radius. Ten pre-production Ki-43s went into flight-testing, and this time the Army evaluators were greatly impressed with the improvements. It was found that the Ki-43 could now be looped and "Immelmanned" at speeds of 168mph or slower, stall recovery and acceleration from low airspeeds were excellent and the "butterfly" flaps produced an astounding rate-of-turn. What the testing did not discover was that Nakajima's efforts to lighten the wing structure had also weakened it, making the wing vulnerable to structural failure in high-G combat maneuvers.

On January 9, 1941, more than three years after Nakajima designers began working on the Ki-43 project, the Army gave approval for production of the Type 1 Fighter Model 1-Ko to begin, and formally bestowed on it the name Hayabusa (Peregrine Falcon). Nakajima's plant at Ota geared up for production, and deliveries of the Ki-43 began in June 1941. Two months later, the 59th and 64th Sentais became the first units to begin converting from the tried-and-true Ki-27 to the new Ki-43. Both units suffered accidents resulting from wing failures during dives, and their remaining fighters were hurriedly modified to rectify the problem. The modification would prove only moderately successful, however.

By November, just weeks before Japan's attack on the US installation at Pearl Harbor, Hawaii, the two Hayabusa units had completed their training and moved to bases in Southeast Asia. They went into action on the first morning of the Pacific War on December 7, and within two weeks they had run up considerable scores of enemy aircraft destroyed in combat over Malaya, Burma and Singapore. Initially, the Allies assumed that all Japanese low-wing radial-engined fighters were Mitsubishi A6M Type 0s, but when it became known that the Ki-43 was indeed an entirely different aircraft, they assigned it the code name "Oscar."

From the outset of production, the JAAF and Nakajima knew that the Ki-43-I would be an interim version of the new fighter. Design work on the definitive model of the Hayabusa began almost immediately, and in February 1942 the first of five prototype Ki-43-IIs rolled out of Nakajima's experimental workshop at Ota.

Although outwardly similar to the previous model, the Ki-43-II featured numerous important upgrades. A new optical gunsight replaced the telescopic sight, modest pilot armor protection was added, the radiator was improved and the wing tips were re-engineered. The wing was strengthened internally, and provisions were added to mount bombs or drop tanks from racks under the wings. Armament was upgraded to two 12.7mm Ho-103 Type 1 machine guns, with 250 rounds of ammunition per weapon, and this would remain standard in all future models of the Hayabusa. At the

The 25th Sentai commenced operations in China with the Ki-43-I in October 1942. This Hayabusa was captured sometime during 1943 and repainted with Chinese markings at Kweilin. The identifying characteristics of the Ki-43-I were the telescopic gunsight, protruding through the windscreen, and the two-bladed propeller. (David Trujillo)

front of the airplane, a redesigned air intake system was routed to the 1,150hp Ha-115 engine, which featured a two-stage supercharger and drove a fixed-pitch, three-blade propeller.

Trials of the new Hayabusa revealed it to be an improvement over the previous model, and the JAAF ordered the fighter into production. In November 1942, the Ki-43-II-Ko began to supplant the Ki-43-I on the assembly line at Ota, gradually claiming a greater share of the production volume until the last Ki-43-I was rolled out in February 1943. The Ki-43-II, in several versions, would go on to become the model of the Hayabusa produced in the greatest numbers. The airplane boasted a top speed of 329mph at 13,125ft, a service ceiling of 36,750ft and a normal range of 1,095 miles. It would fight on every major front of the Pacific War, and also equipped advanced training units in Japan and Southeast Asia.

A final version of the Hayabusa was the Ki-43-III, which appeared in 1944. It is a testament to the decline of Japan's fortunes by this point in the war that the aircraft was produced at all, since the performance of advanced Allied fighters had long since left the nimble Hayabusa far behind. Built mainly by Tachikawa so as to allow Nakajima to concentrate on its superior Ki-84 Hayate fighter, the Ki-43-III mounted a more powerful Ha-115-II engine of 1,190hp, with individual exhaust stacks protruding from the rear of the cowling. The additional power allowed the Ki-43-III to reach a top speed of 358mph at 21,920ft and a service ceiling of 37,400ft, but it remained hindered by its woefully inadequate armament of two machine guns. Tachikawa manufactured close to 1,000 Ki-43-IIIs between October 1944 and June 1945.

The Ki-43 remained in frontline service with the JAAF from the first day of the Pacific War to the last, equipping 36 fighter sentais and numerous independent units for at least part of that time. Although JAAF fighters with better performance were introduced throughout the war, the Ki-43 was still in service with 18 sentais when the conflict finally ended.

TECHNICAL SPECIFICATIONS

CURTISS P-40

P-40/Tomahawk I

Aircraft in the first batch of 199 production P-40s were not truly combat-worthy, as they lacked armor-plating and self-sealing fuel tanks. Fortunately, the US had not yet entered the war when the first P-40s were delivered. Powered by an early version of the Allison V-1710 liquid-cooled V12 engine, the aircraft was fitted with two 0.50-in. machine guns in the nose and one 0.30-in. weapon in each wing. The French ordered a similar model, designated the H-81-A1, which was armed with four 0.30-in. wing guns instead of two. Most of these were taken over by the British as Tomahawk Is in mid-1940 after France fell to the Germans. They were employed by the RAF primarily as trainers, or stored for future shipment overseas.

P-40B-C/Tomahawk II

The first upgrade of the P-40 line addressed many of the shortcomings of the previous model. Improvements included armor protection for the pilot, upgraded radio equipment and the addition of a second 0.30-in. machine gun in each wing. The P-40C added self-sealing fuel tanks and the provision to carry a drop tank or bomb on a centerline station below the cockpit. Many P-40B/Cs found their way to USAAC squadrons in the Philippine Islands and Hawaii, thus becoming the first Warhawks to see action in American markings. The British version of these aircraft, fitted with

0.303-in. wing guns but otherwise similar, was used for low-level fighter-reconnaissance sorties over occupied Europe and in fighter-bomber operations in North Africa. Some 100 aircraft were diverted in 1941 from the British order to the CAF, where they would equip the legendary AVG, soon to be known worldwide as the "Flying Tigers."

P-40D-E/Kittyhawk I

When Allison redesigned its V-1710 to produce the upgraded "F-series" engine, Curtiss needed to redesign the P-40's fuselage to accommodate the higher thrust line and additional horsepower produced by the new motor. With the guns having been removed from the redesigned nose of the P-40D, Curtiss replaced the four small-caliber weapons in the wings with 0.50-in. machine guns in the P-40D. The armament was increased to six 0.50-in. guns in the P-40E, as it was in late-build Kittyhawk Is and all Kittyhawk IAs. The new fuselage also introduced an improved cockpit enclosure, with a bigger windscreen and deeper sliding canopy. The USAAF's P-40E-1 could carry six small bombs under the wings, and late in its production run a small dorsal fillet was added at the base of the vertical stabilizer to improve longitudinal stability. P-40Es and Kittyhawk Is saw extensive combat in the Pacific and CBI theaters, and in North Africa from 1941.

P-40F/Kittyhawk II

In an attempt to improve the performance of the P-40 at higher altitudes, Curtiss fitted an E-model airframe with a Rolls-Royce Merlin engine – the same powerplant as in the Spitfire and Hurricane. The engine, license-built by the Packard Motor Co and equipped with the two-stage mechanical supercharger, gave the P-40F a top speed of 364mph at 20,000ft. The nose was redesigned to remove the air scoop atop the cowling because the Merlin engine had an updraft carburetor. Instead, the engine drew its air through an enlarged radiator scoop below the engine. In a further effort to improve the stability of the Warhawk, Curtiss extended the rear of the fuselage by 26in., starting with the 700th P-40F.

An oxcart passes a line of Warhawks on a Chinese airfield in early 1944. The P-40K closest to the camera ("400" *DUKE*) was assigned to Maj Bob Liles, commanding officer of the 16th FS/51st FG and an ace with five victories to his credit. The other Warhawks are from the 26th FS/51st FG. (Jack Muller)

Because they were considered better able to cope with high-flying German and Italian fighters, most P-40Fs and Kittyhawk IIs were sent to American and Commonwealth squadrons fighting in the Mediterranean Theater of Operations (MTO).

P-40K/Kittyhawk III

Outwardly, the P-40K-1 and K-5 Warhawks were identical to the late-production P-40E-1, with the small dorsal fillet at the base of the vertical stabilizer and flared exhaust pipes fitted to the engine. But there was a big difference under the cowling; Curtiss gave the P-40K a considerable boost in power over previous Allison-engined models with the 1,325hp V-1710-73. The armament remained six 0.50-in. guns in the wings. The added power made the P-40K the fastest Warhawk yet, even slightly outpacing the P-40F at 20,000ft. The additional speed was not wasted on its pilots. No less a proponent of the airplane than Col Bruce K. Holloway – a 13-victory ace over China with the 23rd FG – considered the P-40K his favorite Warhawk because it delivered improved performance without compromising flight characteristics or combat equipment.

With the P-40K-10/15, Curtiss went to the 26-in. fuselage extension introduced with the late-model P-40F. These were the first P-40s fitted with a radio antenna mast on the fuselage spine. The RAF received 192 Kittyhawk IIIs through Lend-Lease, with most of them being assigned to Commonwealth air forces.

P-40L/Kittyhawk II

Seeing no further prospects for a significant boost in engine power any time soon, Curtiss began to strip weight from the Warhawk in the P-40L. This model was basically a Merlin-powered P-40F with several items removed or modified. Armament was reduced to four 0.50-in. wing guns, less armor plate was fitted and internal fuel capacity dropped from 157 gal to 120 gal. These changes lopped about 140lb from

In the spring of 1944, a USAAF technical team from Eglin Field, Florida, came to China to introduce P-40 squadrons to the use of aerial rockets against ground targets. Here, a P-40N of the 25th FS/51st FG is fitted with three-tube rocket launchers and practice bombs in preparation for a training mission. (Stan Strout)

the empty weight, compared to the P-40F. A very slight improvement in performance over the F-model resulted, but the loss of combat effectiveness more than offset the gain in speed. The P-40L-1 retained the short fuselage of the early P-40F, but the 650 P-40Ls with serial numbers starting at 42-10480 had the 26-in. fuselage extension. The P-40Ls supplied to the RAF were designated Kittyhawk IIs, as were the P-40Fs.

As the end of the P-40F/L production run drew near in spring 1943, the USAAF decided that the new North American P-51B fighter should have the top priority for Merlin engines. This decision left 300 P-40F/L airframes lacking engines, and these were converted to Allison power and redesignated P-40Rs.

P-40M/Kittyhawk III

Throughout the P-40's life, Curtiss was trying to develop a new fighter to replace the Warhawk in production. The Curtiss P-46 and P-60 designs failed to pan out, however, and the USAAF still needed fighters. An order for 600 new P-40M Warhawks resulted, with deliveries starting in November 1942. Outwardly, the P-40M

Crewmen fit a new propeller to a P-40N in the hangar at Kunming. As the last production model of the Warhawk, the N-model featured a 1,200hp Allison V-1710-81 engine, an improved cockpit enclosure with a clear sliding canopy and cut-down rear deck, and smaller main landing gear wheels made of lightweight magnesium, which lacked hubcaps. (Leon Klesman)

was little changed from the long-tailed P-40K, but it was powered by the new 1,200hp Allison V-1710-81. This engine could draw bypass air for the carburetor through metal filters fed by a perforated grill on each side of the nose ahead of the exhausts. A further visual clue was the addition of a vent window in the port side of the windscreen. Another new feature was reinforced, although still fabric-covered, ailerons. The P-40M-5 introduced a permanent carburetor air filter for the engine, and a new feature on the P-40M-10 was a mechanically-operated landing gear indicator on each wing. Because the P-40M was so similar to the P-40K, the RAF designated both aircraft Kittyhawk IIIs.

P-40N/Kittyhawk IV

The last production version of the Warhawk, the P-40N was a further attempt to cut weight from the veteran fighter. In all, 5,210 P-40Ns were built in nine sub-versions, making it the most numerous of all Warhawks, and also the most varied. The first version, the P-40N-1, was outwardly similar to the P-40M except that its armament was reduced to four wing guns. It also featured the smaller internal fuel capacity of 120 gal. Another weight saving resulted from the elimination of the battery, but this meant that the airplane had to be started by an external power source, which caused headaches for combat units operating the fighter in forward areas. Most P-40Ns were retrofitted with batteries as a result.

Powered by a 1,200hp Allison V-1710-81 engine, the P-40N-1 was the fastest Warhawk, with a top speed of 378mph at 20,000ft. An improved cockpit enclosure, with a clear sliding canopy and cut-down rear deck, debuted on the P-40N-5 to give the pilot a better view out of the airplane. The main landing gear got smaller wheels made of lightweight magnesium and lacking hubcaps. In China, where supplies and spare parts were severely limited, the switch to the new wheels caused problems for the Fourteenth Air Force because the gravel runways there wore out tires in a hurry, and the stockpiled replacement tires for older P-40s would not fit the smaller-diameter wheels.

On the plus side, the P-40N-5 reverted to six wing guns, and improvements were made to the pilot's seat and the radio equipment. The 100 P-40N-10s were winterized versions of the N-5, and were the first to include a rate-of-climb indicator among the instruments. Internal fuel capacity grew to 161 gal in the P-40N-15, and the P-40N-20 got a new engine in the form of the 1360hp V-1710-99, along with pylons under each wing that could carry a bomb of up to 500lb in weight or a drop tank. Minor changes continued in the P-40N-25, -30 and -35, and the last production Warhawk, the P-40N-40, was the first with metal-skinned ailerons.

Most of the 458 Lend-Lease Kittyhawk IVs went to New Zealand and Australia for service in the Pacific, although some saw action with RAF squadrons in the MTO.

P-40E/N WARHAWK

The Warhawk, from the P-40E through to the P-40N, was fitted with Browning M-2 0.50-in. machine guns, two or three in each wing. The guns were aimed slightly inward so that their streams of fire would converge at a point about 300 yards ahead of the airplane.

NAKAJIMA Ki-43 OSCAR

Ki-43-I

The initial production version of the Hayabusa (Peregrine Falcon), the Ki-43-Ia, featured a 980hp Ha-25 Type 99 14-cylinder radial engine with a single-speed supercharger. A fixed-pitch, two-blade wooden propeller soon gave way to a variable-pitch metal propeller, also with two blades. The wingspan was 37ft 6.3in., with wing area of 237 sq. ft. Armament consisted of two 7.7mm type 89 machine guns in the upper cowling, aimed by a telescope-type gunsight protruding through the windscreen. As supplies of the new 12.7mm Ho-103 machine gun started to become available, one of the 7.7mm guns was replaced by the heavier weapon in the Ki-43-Ib.

When the Pacific War broke out in December 1941, only 40 of these machines had been delivered to combat units. Weakness in the wing spars of the early Hayabusas was only partly remedied by a modification program, and a number of them crashed when the wings collapsed as pilots were pulling out of high-speed dives. A further upgrade to the Hayabusa, the Ki-43-Ic, standardized the armament at two Ho-103 machine guns with 250 rounds per gun, and added attachment points for small bombs or drop tanks under each wing. Of the 716 Ki-43-Is manufactured, all but the first 80 were built to the -Ic specification. The slight addition in weight produced by the heavier guns had little, if any, appreciable effect on the performance of the aircraft.

Ki-43-II

Five prototypes of this first major improvement to the Hayabusa were delivered to the JAAF beginning in February 1942, and by October the new model was in full

Ki-43-II OSCAR

The Ki-43-II was fitted with two Ho-103 Type 1 12.7mm machine guns mounted in the forward fuselage and synchronized to fire through the propeller arc. The butts of the guns extended back into the cockpit on either side of the instrument panel, and the individual magazines for each weapon carried 250 rounds apiece. The Ho-103 was very similar in design to the Browning M-2.

production as the Ki-43-IIa. Further modifications to the wing cured it of its tendency to collapse under high loading, shortening the span by 23.6in. and increasing the load-carrying capacity of the wing racks. The fighter was fitted with the more powerful 1,130hp Nakajima Ha-115 radial engine (which also used a two-speed supercharger) driving a three-bladed metal propeller. The engine was housed in a new cowling that was longer in chord and bigger in diameter, and also featured an air intake for the supercharger in the upper lip. Other improvements included a slightly taller windscreen and canopy, a more effective reflector gunsight, armor plating to protect the pilot and a rubber coating to protect the fuel tanks.

An oil cooler was fitted under the fuselage at the rear of the cowling. The armament, and the Type 96 Hi-3 radio, were unchanged from the previous model. Various minor modifications incorporated during the production run of the Ki-43-IIa were standardized in the Ki-43-IIb, and deliveries began during the summer of 1943. Other changes included a deeper "honeycomb" oil cooler under the cowling, a revised air intake for the carburetor and

Groundcrew of the 25th Sentai perform maintenance on a Ki-43 in China. Note the heavily mottled camouflage scheme on the uppersurfaces and the yellow combat stripe on the leading edge of the wing, extending onto the landing gear cover. (Yasuho Izawa)

an auxiliary cooler intake beneath the fuselage. Later, the hard points under the wing were moved outboard of the landing gear to prevent bombs from striking the propeller during diving attacks. A further development, designated the Ki-43-IIc (also called Ki-43-II KAI), introduced ejector exhaust stubs that gave the engine a slight boost in horsepower.

Ki-43-III

Though the Hayabusa was clearly suffering at the hands of more advanced Allied fighters by the middle of 1944, a new version was nevertheless introduced in the form of the Ki-43-IIIa. Outwardly, it was very similar to the Ki-43-IIc, but its engine was the new Ha-115-II rated at 1,190hp. Tachikawa built 1,098 examples of the Ki-43-IIIa and two prototypes of the Ki-43-IIIb. Fitted with two 20mm cannon and a more powerful Mitsubishi Ha-112-32/42 engine, the Ki-43-IIIc was intended to serve in the home islands as a B-29 interceptor, but the war ended before it could enter production.

A VIEW FROM THE COCKPIT

As the products of two vastly different design specifications, the Ki-43 and P-40 gave their pilots predictably different flight characteristics. With its light weight and relatively large wing, the Ki-43 was a delight to fly. It could "climb like an angel and turn like the devil." The heavy P-40 struck many pilots as truck-like, with a slow rate-of-climb and a marked drop-off in performance at higher altitudes. But the weight also gave it spectacular speed in a dive.

The tactics devised by Fourteenth Air Force commander Claire Chennault for his P-40 pilots in China took advantage of the fighter's strong points – speed, strength and firepower – while attempting to negate its weaknesses. Chennault's P-40 "drivers" learned to attack in a slashing dive through the enemy formation, then zoom up to make another attack. Under no circumstance were they to follow a Ki-43 in a turn or climb. The P-40's heavy armament of six 0.50-in. machine guns constituted a key advantage, as although the 12.7mm Ho-103s carried by the Ki-43 packed virtually the same punch as the Browning guns in the Curtiss fighter, the Oscar only had two of them. So an accurate two-second burst from a P-40 would hit the Ki-43 with 16.2lb of "slugs," which was triple the throw weight that a Ki-43 pilot could bring to bear on a Warhawk.

Outgunned as he was, the Hayabusa pilot needed superior marksmanship to score a kill, and he definitely wanted to avoid a head-on confrontation with a P-40. Finally, the superior firepower of the P-40 also made it much more effective than the Ki-43 at bringing down enemy bombers.

As in any match-up of two fighter aircraft, the advantage could go either way depending on the skill of the pilots and the situation in which combat was joined. A pilot – Japanese or American – looking down from 15,000ft and seeing a formation of enemy fighters in front of him was in a great position to attack. But the success of that attack depended on getting close enough to open fire before the adversary had

16th FS/51st FG crew chief Sgt Ward McMillen perches on the wing of a P-40N-15 while a fresh Allison engine is winched into place. Outdoor maintenance such as this was a fact of life in China. This airplane was the regular mount of Capt Dexter Baumgardner, who was credited with damaging a Ki-43 and probably destroying two Japanese bombers on December 18, 1943 over Kunming. (Tom Glasgow)

27

P-40E/N WARHAWK COCKPIT

1. N-3A Reflector gun sight
2. Ring gun sight
3. Flap and wheel indicator
4. Compass
5. Flight indicator
6. Coolant temperature gauge
7. Fuselage fuel gauge
8. Turn and bank indicator
9. Turn indicator
10. Airspeed indicator
11. Tachometer
12. Manifold pressure gauge
13. Oil temperature gauge
14. Engine gauge unit

15. Rate of climb indicator
16. Altimeter
17. Oxygen indicator
18. Oxygen pressure gauge
19. Oil pressure gauge
20. Fuel pressure gauge
21. Parking brake
22. Gun arming switch
23. Warning lights
24. Carburetor heat control
25. Canopy control crank
26. Throttle
27. Mixture control

28. Propeller control
29. Ignition switch
30. Compass control
31. Ammeter
32. Cockpit heat control
33. Rudder trim tab control
34. Elevator trim tab control
35. Fuel selector
36. Rudder pedals
37. Control column
38. Gun firing button
39. Forward wing tank fuel gauge
40. Hydraulics hand pump

41. Radio receiver
42. Radio transmitter
43. Map case
44. Fluorescent spotlight
45. Wing bomb release
46. Pilot's seat
47. Cowl flaps control
48. Radio crash switch
49. Filter switch box
50. Fluorescent spotlight
51. Oxygen regulator
52. Oxygen hose
53. Flap selector
54. U/C selector handle

Ki-43 OSCAR COCKPIT

1. Gun sight
2. Airspeed indicator
3. Turn and bank indicator
4. Rate of climb indicator
5. Manifold pressure gauge
6. Compass
7. Altimeter
8. Tachometer
9. Fuel pressure gauge
10. Oil pressure gauge
11. Oil temperature gauge
12. U/C warning lights
13. 12.77mm gun

14. Guarded switch cover
15. Engine primer fuel pump
16. Cocking handle
17. Cabin lamp
18. Elevator trimming
19. Chronometer
20. Radio tuner
21. Radio dial
22. Cylinder temperature
23. Exhaust temperature
24. Control column
25. Canopy winding

mechanism
26. Combat flap control buttons
27. Main switches
28. Oxygen control
29. Oxygen flow meter
30. Fuel gauge (main tanks)
31. Fuel gauge (auxiliary tanks)
32. Right and left auxiliary tank selector
33. Right and left main

tank selector
34. Pilot's seat
35. Hydrostatic plunger for main tanks
36. Hydrostatic plunger for auxiliary tanks
37. Hydraulic brake pedals
38. Rudder pedals
39. P.4 compass
40. Emergency hydraulics hand pump
41. Magneto switch
42. Throttle lever

43. Mixture control
44. Propeller pitch control
45. Friction adjuster
46. Control handle valve (use unknown)
47. Internal tanks cock
48. Main fuel cock
49. U/C emergency operation
50. Cam manipulation
51. U/C selector
52. Flap selector
53. Compressed air bottle

a chance to take evasive action. An alert Ki-43 pilot attacked from the rear by a P-40 could use his superior maneuverability to turn or loop out of the line of fire, while a P-40 pilot in the same situation could push over into a dive and quickly outdistance the Ki-43. In this situation, the advantage went to the Ki-43, because it could maneuver at any altitude. The P-40 needed sufficient altitude in order to dive away, and if caught "low and slow," it was likely to take a pounding.

On the other hand, the Ki-43 mounted a high-pressure oxygen cylinder behind the pilot's seat that had a nasty habit of exploding if struck by enemy fire, tearing the Hayabusa to pieces. The P-40's tough frame could absorb a lot of punishment, and its cooling system was mounted under the engine in the nose – a difficult spot to hit from behind.

With their opposite strengths and weaknesses, the Ki-43 and P-40 fit together like two pieces of a puzzle. But the bottom line was this. No Ki-43 pilot wanted to trade his Hayabusa for a P-40, and even if he did, he would not have found a Warhawk pilot willing to make the swap.

P-40 AND Ki-43 COMPARISON SPECIFICATIONS		
	P-40N-15	**Ki-43-II**
Powerplant	1,200hp V-1710-81	1,105hp Ha-115
Dimensions		
Span	37ft 3.5in.	35ft 6.75in.
Length	33ft 5.75in.	29ft 3.25in.
Height	12ft 4.5in.	10ft 8.75in.
Wing area	236 sq. ft	230.37 sq. ft
Weights		
Empty	6,200lb	3,812lb
Loaded	8,350lb	4,891lb
Wing loading	35.38lb/sq. ft	21.23lb/sq. ft
Performance		
Max speed	343 mph at 15,000ft	329 mph at 13,125ft
Range	750 miles	1,006 miles
Climb	to 14,000ft in 7.3 min.	to 19,685ft in 6.35 min.
Service ceiling	31,000ft	36,794ft
Armament	6 x 0.50-in. Brownings	2 x 12.7mm Ho-103s

THE STRATEGIC SITUATION

Starting in early 1942, the P-40 and Ki-43 met in combat at various locations throughout the Pacific theater, primarily in the savage skies above New Guinea, Burma and China. These clashes reached maximum intensity during the Japanese *Ichi-Go* land offensive in China during 1944.

Although conventional history tells us the Pacific War started with Japan's attack on Pearl Harbor on December 7, 1941, the roots of the conflict go back a full decade further to September 1931, when the Japanese Kwantung Army invaded the Manchuria region of northeast China. Seeking to expand its industrial capacity, Japan occupied Manchurian cities, took over the railways and installed a puppet government. The Chinese retaliated by boycotting Japanese goods, sparking a six-week clash between Chinese and Japanese troops in early 1932 that became known as the "Shanghai Incident." Five years of relative calm followed, during which time both nations built up their military forces – including their air arms – in expectation of future conflict.

On July 7, 1937, fighting again erupted between Japan and China, this time at the Marco Polo Bridge on the outskirts of Peking, and soon spread throughout northern China. By this time, nearly all of China's warlords had submitted to the central authority of Generalissimo Chiang Kai-shek's Kuomintang government, and a flourishing Communist movement had been bottled up in a remote area of northern China. For the next eight years China would be gripped in a state of full-scale war.

JAAF fighter units, flying Kawasaki Ki-10 biplanes, quickly gained air superiority over Chinese pilots equipped with foreign-built aircraft such as the Curtiss Hawk II

P-40Ns of the 5th FG CACW on the line at Chihkiang in 1944. The aircraft in the foreground ("765" of the 17th FS) carries a drop tank under the centerline and clusters of fragmentation bombs on its wing racks. Note the chalked-in sharksmouth on the second Warhawk in the line. (Bill Mustill)

fighter and Northrop 2E light bomber. Poorly trained and haphazardly employed, the CAF suffered devastating losses. Even the hiring of retired US Army Capt Claire L. Chennault, a noted pilot and expert on fighter tactics, as an advisor to the CAF failed to change the situation.

Chennault's efforts to buy modern aircraft and train Chinese pilots to fly them were frustrated by China's rigid class system and the rampant corruption in Chiang's government. Occasionally, the CAF was able to launch effective interceptions against Japanese raiders, but these ultimately failed to slow the constantly advancing enemy. First Peking was captured, then Shanghai and Nanking. When Chiang's government moved inland to Hankow, Japanese bombers followed. In late 1938, when Hankow fell to the Japanese, the Kuomintang government retreated farther into central China, settling in the city of Chungking, on the Yangtze River.

The Chinese were finally able to stop the advancing Japanese in May 1939 at Tsaoyang, in mountainous Hupeh Province. As a stalemate ensued, the Japanese turned to a strategy of attrition. They blockaded China's coastal ports to prevent much-needed supplies from reaching the interior, and supplied their own ground forces with indigenous Chinese resources. At the same time, Japanese bombers continued to attack the cities of free China, including the new capital. Millions of civilians died.

The outbreak of war in Europe in September 1939 only worsened China's situation. When France surrendered to Germany, an ally of Japan, on 22 June 1940, the port of Hanoi, in French Indo-China (now Vietnam), was closed to supplies bound for China. The only port of entry left for China-bound goods was Rangoon, in the British colony of Burma. From there, supplies could be shipped north by rail to the new "Burma Road," and on into China. Chennault feared that China could lose this route as well if Japan and Great Britain went to war, which was looking increasingly likely, unless the Burma Road could be defended from air attack. Further, he had concluded by this time that the current CAF would not be up to the task.

Chennault and Chiang were able to convince US President Franklin D. Roosevelt to provide China with 100 American military pilots and frontline fighters for them to fly in defense of the Burma Road. The AVG formed in the summer of 1941 on a jungle airfield at Toungoo, in Burma, and immediately began training on Curtiss 81-A2 Tomahawks that had been hastily diverted from a British order for the export version of the P-40.

By coincidence, it was also during this time that the 59th and 64th sentais of the JAAF became the first units to re-equip with the new Ki-43-I. As tensions between Japan and the US grew in the weeks preceding the Pearl Harbor attack, the 59th and 64th sentais were deployed to the Malay Peninsula, while the Third Pursuit Squadron of the AVG went to Rangoon, thus setting up the first aerial duel between the P-40 and the Ki-43.

After a successful interception over Rangoon by AVG and RAF fighters on December 23, 1941, the 64th Sentai was ordered north from Malaya to bolster the escort force for a second bombing raid against Rangoon on Christmas Day. Led by Sentai Commander Maj Tateo Kato, 25 Ki-43s of the 64th met 63 Ki-21 heavy bombers over Thailand and proceeded with them west toward Rangoon. The formation eventually came apart en route, however, and Kato's Ki-43s were split into two forces.

As the Japanese aircraft crossed into Burma, two flights (totaling 13 AVG P-40s) took off from Mingladon airfield, along with a similar number of RAF Brewster Buffalo fighters. The opposing forces duly fought a huge aerial battle that raged for

The CAF operated Curtiss Hawk biplane fighters, which were export versions of the US Navy's F11C Goshawk, during the late 1930s. These aircraft enjoyed occasional success against JAAF and JNAF biplane fighters, but they were no match for the Ki-27 when the latter made its combat debut in China in 1938. This Hawk, assigned to a rear-area airfield near Chengtu, somehow survived in CAF service through to 1944. (Barry Corfman)

about 30 minutes while the Japanese formation was withdrawing across the Gulf of Martaban. One of the AVG pilots, flight leader William N. Reed of Marion, Iowa, made several firing runs at the bombers before being forced to dive away from the fight to clear his guns after they had jammed. Reed duly described what happened next in his diary:

> I saw another P-40 who was also leaving the scrap. By now we were 140-150 miles across the gulf from Rangoon. I joined the other ship and saw that it was (Parker) Dupouy. We started back across the gulf at 17,000ft, and had only gone about 30 miles out off the shore of Moulmein when we spotted three Model Os (actually Ki-43s, which were unknown to the AVG at this time) in a V-formation below us, apparently heading home. We dropped down on their tails and surprised them. Dupouy was following me as I picked out the right-hand wingman. I fired from about 50 yards, and Dupouy fired behind me. The Jap exploded right in front of my face. I pulled sharply up to the right to avoid hitting him, and Dupouy pulled up to the left. In doing so, his right wing clipped the other Jap wingman's ship right in the wing root, and the Jap spun into the gulf, too.

As far as can be determined, Reed and Dupouy had scored the first two P-40 victories over the Ki-43, although they did not know it at the time. Many of the AVG P-40s were hit in the fight, and two pilots made wheels-up landings at an auxiliary airstrip, but it is not known whether they were victims of Ki-43s or other Japanese aircraft involved in the battle. In any case, it was a spectacular start to the long and bitter rivalry between the two fighter types.

When Burma fell to the Japanese five months later, the AVG withdrew to China. Now the only lifeline left for China was a slender stream of goods that could be flown into the country from India over the mountainous route that became known as the "Hump." The AVG provided air defense for Chinese cities and the "Hump" route, while also supporting Chinese forces attempting to prevent the Japanese from advancing across the Salween River into China's Yunnan Province. When the AVG was disbanded in July 1942, USAAF pilots of the new CATF took over its mission, and what remained of its tired P-40s.

Although the CATF was a small force consisting of just five P-40 squadrons and one B-25 medium-bomber unit, Chennault (now a USAAF brigadier general) had prepared well to carry on the fight. Not only had he convinced the Chinese to build an extensive network of airfields from which the CATF could operate, he had also engineered a vast "warning net" of civilian spotters who could quickly alert Warhawk units to the presence of incoming Japanese air attacks from virtually anywhere in unoccupied China.

Chennault's headquarters for the CATF was located at Kunming, in Yunnan province, as it had been for the AVG. Kunming was also the air terminal for cargo flying over the "Hump," as it was located about as far into China as a heavily loaded transport airplane could fly from India and still maintain a safe reserve of fuel. From Kunming, a string of airfields stretched northeastward some 600 miles to Hengyang, with others along the way at Kweilin and Lingling. To the north, airfields in the vicinity of Chungking hosted units of the CAF whose primary duty was to provide air defense for the capital.

For their part, the Japanese surrounded the CATF on three sides. The JAAF maintained air bases in the Hankow area to the northeast, at Canton and Hong Kong, on the China coast, and to the south in French Indo-China and northern Burma. The JAAF did not, however, have aircraft in sufficient strength to maintain offensive operations from all of these places at the same time.

A sort of cat-and-mouse war ensued therefore, with commanders on both sides moving their air units regularly to take advantage of weather conditions, supplies and/or tactical considerations. Keeping sufficient supplies of ammunition and fuel on hand to maintain operations was a constant struggle for the Americans, as all of their material had to be flown into China over the "Hump." Bad weather, enemy action and even political decisions could cut the "Hump" flow to a trickle – and often did.

Aerial clashes between the CATF's 23rd FG and the JAAF over China began immediately after the AVG dissolved on July 4, 1942. Operating

The Chinese Army provided security on Fourteenth Air Force air bases in China. Here, a shoeless young soldier guards a P-40N of the 74th FS at Kweilin. Under-equipped and often poorly led, the Chinese fell back before the powerful Japanese forces that took part in the *Ichi-Go* offensive. (Leon Klesman)

primarily from the eastern bases, the P-40s initially maintained a defensive posture as the JAAF, flying from Hankow and Canton, attempted to wipe out the novice American pilots. A small cadre of former AVG aviators had remained in China, however, and these men provided the leadership and combat savvy needed to hold the line while the newly arrived USAAF pilots gained experience.

By late October, Chennault had built up sufficient strength to undertake substantial offensive operations. His first targets were the dock areas on the Kowloon peninsula, which B-25s, escorted by P-40s of the 23rd FG, struck on October 25, 1942. An even bigger raid hit the port facilities at Canton in November. The Japanese struck back on December 26 and again in mid-January 1943, both times sending bombers from Burma to attack the "Hump" airfield at Yunnanyi, in southwest China.

When the Fourteenth Air Force succeeded the CATF in spring 1943, it signaled the beginning of a build-up of American air power in China. By early 1944, Chennault would have at his disposal four fighter groups equipped with P-40s (the USAAF 23rd and 51st FGs and the 3rd and 5th FGs of the Chinese-American Composite Wing), a P-38 fighter squadron, two medium bomb groups with B-25s and a heavy bomb group flying B-24 Liberators.

With these aircraft, Chennault was able not only to maintain pressure on the Japanese land forces in China through steady attacks on their lines of communication, but also to harass Japanese shipping carrying vital war materials from Southeast Asia to Japan through the South China Sea. In late 1943, Chennault reorganized his forces into the 68th Composite Wing (CW) on the eastern front and the 69th CW, covering the "Hump" route from bases in southwest China. In addition, squadrons of the newly formed Chinese-American Composite Wing (CACW) were arriving in China sporadically as they completed combat training in India.

To keep pace, the JAAF upgraded its 3rd Air Division, concentrated in the Hankow area, to the 5th Air Army in January 1944. This enlarged force now included two Ki-43 sentais (the 25th and 48th), two interceptor sentais with short-range Ki-44s and various bombing and army cooperation units.

The run of defeats for Japanese forces in the South Pacific during 1943, coupled with the growing Allied strength on the Asian mainland, prompted its high command to respond with plans for a major land offensive in China. The express aim of this attack, codenamed *Ichi-Go* ('Number One'), was to drive the Fourteenth Air Force out of its eastern air bases and, if possible, force China out of the war. This would prevent long-range B-29 bombers from using Chinese bases in future raids on targets in the Japanese home islands. An added benefit would be the establishment of a rail link all the way from Hanoi to Shanghai, the great port city on China's east coast. This would allow vital war materials from Southeast Asia to bypass the increasingly dangerous sea routes on their way to Japan.

As early as January 1944, Chinese intelligence noted a build-up of Japanese land forces in the Hankow area and north of the Yellow River. Then, on April 17, 1944, Japanese troops under the command of Gen Shunroku Hada began pouring across the Yellow River at Kaifeng and heading south through Honan Province along the rail corridor to Hankow, some 250 miles away. At the same time, other Japanese forces

pushed north from Hankow on the same route in this first phase of *Ichi-Go*. Their aim was to close this last gap in the railway line between Peking and Hankow, thus opening a new route for the flow of men and supplies south for the second phase of *Ichi-Go*, which was soon to follow.

Chennault responded by moving the four P-40 squadrons of the 3rd FG CACW, plus a CACW B-25 squadron, north to air bases in eastern Szechwan Province. From there they could launch attacks on the advancing Japanese in an effort called "Mission A." Bad weather hampered the transfer, and it was not until April 30 that the CACW was able to launch its first sorties of the campaign. By that time, the two Japanese forces were well on their way toward linking up, which they soon did. From that point on, the "Mission A" forces would pound the Peking-Hankow rail corridor constantly, seeking to deny the Japanese use of it. Skirmishes between CACW P-40s and Ki-43s of the 5th Air Army became routine.

Meanwhile, the bigger picture of the Japanese battle plan became apparent to Chennault and his Fourteenth Air Force staff. The 68th CW received orders to launch attacks on the Hankow area with the aim of destroying Japanese supplies before they could be used in the second phase of *Ichi-Go*. The first mission went off as planned on May 6, with a strong force of 54 bombers and fighters led by 23rd FG CO Col David L. "Tex" Hill attacking a supply depot near the the main Hankow airfield with moderate success.

The Japanese responded in kind, with the Fifth Air Army launching a series of attacks against USAAF air bases in eastern China with the goal of gaining air superiority over the area so the Americans would be unable to disrupt the offensive.

Neither the American effort to cripple the build-up nor the Japanese bid for air superiority succeeded, however. On May 26, 1944, when 60,000 assault troops of the Japanese Eleventh Army marched south out of Hankow toward the Chinese-held city of Changsha, their first objective, the 68th CW, immediately started pounding them from the skies. The *Ichi-Go* Offensive, which would provide the backdrop for the last major confrontation involving the P-40 and the Ki-43, was now under way.

Ki-43-II "15" of the 2nd Chutai/25th Sentai taxis at Nanking. Its pilot is SgtMaj Kyushiro Ohtake, a ten-victory ace who flew operationally from March 1941 through to the end of the war. Seriously wounded in combat over Seoul on August 13, 1945, he eventually succumbed to his injuries in 1951. (Yasuho Izawa)

THE COMBATANTS

Just as the P-40 and Ki-43 differed according to the attitudes and philosophies of the nations that produced them, so did the pilots who flew these legendary fighters. The United States and Japan were two vastly different places in the 1940s, each with cultures and traditions that seemed incomprehensible to the other. The United States was a young democracy, not yet 200 years old, founded on the principles of "life, liberty and the pursuit of happiness." Japan, in contrast, was an ancient land bound in a strict class structure and ruled by its military.

It was only natural that the young men of these two countries would approach military service with different mindsets, although they certainly shared patriotic dedication to their respective homelands.

PILOT TRAINING

Aviation held a great attraction for young men of both nations during the years leading up to the Pearl Harbor attack, thanks in no small part to the heroic portrayals of World War I aces and the subsequent aerial adventures of pilots such as Charles Lindbergh and Jimmy Doolittle. Because of that, the Japanese and American air forces were able to set high standards for intelligence and physical condition in their pilot recruits.

As might be expected, the training programs of the JAAF and USAAF were similar in structure. After completing preparatory military training, which could last for several months, student pilots began flying lessons in primary school on docile training aircraft – mostly biplanes such as the Stearman PT-17 (US) and Tachikawa Ki-17

(Japan). One of the main purposes of primary training was to weed out those who showed no talent for flying, but the students who graduated went on to the next level, called "basic" training in the US and "advanced" in Japan. Here, the standard training aircraft for American Army pilots was the Vultee BT-13/15, a low-wing monoplane with fixed landing gear, while Japanese cadets flew Tachikawa Ki-9 biplanes.

American Army trainees flew the much-admired North American AT-6, a monoplane with retractable landing gear, in their final training phases, called "advanced." The final phase for JAAF pilots was known as "operational" training, in which pilots flew the Tachikawa Ki-55, a low-wing monoplane with fixed landing gear that doubled as an Army cooperation aircraft.

Despite these similarities, there were three important differences in the two nations' pilot training programs. The first was flight time. An American pilot would receive his wings and officer's commission after about nine months of instruction and 200 hours of flight time. In prewar years, he would then be assigned to an active squadron, where his piloting skills would continue to develop while flying first-line combat aircraft. In December 1942, the USAAF instituted Fighter Replacement Training Units (FRTUs) to give newly minted fighter pilots experience in the types of aircraft they would be flying in combat. The FRTU courses (normally some two months in duration) included instrument training and night flying, air-to-air and air-to-ground gunnery instruction and practice in formation flying and combat maneuvering.

JAAF fighter pilots who finished primary training were assigned to a Kyoiku Hiko-tai (flying training unit) for six months. Then they were posted to a fighter sentai, where an additional three months of training were undertaken prior to entering combat. The Japanese fighter pilot could therefore enter combat with more flight time – some 300 hours over two years – than his American counterpart. The JAAF did not see a need for all of its pilots to be officers, however, and as a result all but the few trainees chosen for officer status began their flying careers as enlisted men.

While new Hayabusas were still being shipped to combat units in China and elsewhere, older Ki-43s such as these were pressed into duty as advanced trainers in Japan. With its docile nature and exemplary flying characteristics, the Ki-43 was ideal in that role. (Craig Busby)

Pilots of the 1st Chutai/25th Sentai pose for a group photograph. They are, in the front row from left to right, Tominaga, Osawa and Kimura, and the second row, from left to right, Murakami, Lt Masao Okumura, Capt Takashi Tsuchiya (1st Chutai leader), unknown, Saito and WO Eiji Seino (an ace with an estimated ten victories). (Yasuho Izawa)

The balance in flight training would tip dramatically once the US and Japan went to war against each other, however. The Americans held tight to their 200-hour syllabus throughout the war, considering this the minimum amount of training needed for a military pilot to achieve his wings. But the JAAF did not have this luxury. After the Allies began to gain the upper hand in the Pacific in mid-1942, shortages of fuel and equipment, plus the demand for replacement pilots on the war fronts, made it increasingly difficult for the JAAF to maintain the quality of its flight instruction. By 1944, fledgling JAAF pilots were being sent into combat with a pitiful 60 to 70 hours of flight experience, and the results were predictable.

A striking difference between USAAF and JAAF training was the intensity and methods of imposing discipline on their respective student pilots. Both air forces recognized the need to establish military order and teach respect for the chain of command among their pilots, but they diverged on the methods for doing so.

The Americans took a somewhat casual approach to training, with classroom instruction in military conduct supplemented by relatively gentle "hazing" from training instructors and senior student pilots. Punishments for infractions – forgetting to salute a superior or failing an inspection, for instance – were likely to be assignments to some of the unsavory tasks connected with military service, such as guard duty and kitchen clean-up. Since the goal of most student pilots was to graduate from flight school and become a military pilot, the threat of expulsion was all the motivation most cadets needed to learn the rules, and observe them.

Japanese military training was altogether different in this regard, seeking to instill total dedication to the Emperor and to Japan in its fighting men, along with complete disregard for one's self-interest. As had been the case for centuries, the Japanese were taught that they would gain greatest honor by dying for their country, with a complete disdain for suffering, surrender or death. A key element in teaching this to young men, mostly in their teens, was corporal punishment. JAAF pilot Yasuo Kuwahara described his thoughts on this topic in his book *Kamikaze*:

Military men, regardless of nationality, follow the same basic rules. The great difference lay in how these rules were enforced. An American, for example, who failed to be clean shaven or to have his shoes properly shined for an inspection might have his pass revoked for a day or two, or he might be given extra duty. For us, however, as for all of Nippon's basic trainees, the slightest infraction, the most infinitesimal mistake, brought excruciating punishment.

What I can only describe as a siege of ruthless discipline and relentless castigation began in the first hours of our arrival, and thereafter never ceased during all the days of our training – a siege so terrible that some did not survive it. No matter how perfectly we performed our tasks, the "hancho" (training instructor) found excuses to make us suffer. Punishment was an integral part of our training, and served two main purposes – to create unwavering discipline and to develop an invincible fighting spirit.

For all of us it was a question not merely of learning skills but of survival. Anyone who could withstand the "hancho" would never run from the enemy, and would prefer death to surrender. Whether this policy really produced a superior fighting man, I am not prepared to say. Courage may have more than one connotation. Nonetheless, it did create men who were either so fearless or so dedicated that they would almost invariably fight to the death.

BELOW LEFT
P-40 squadrons in China employed the "finger four" flight formation, which had originally been devised by the Luftwaffe during the Spanish Civil War. This formation, where aircraft flew in positions roughly equal to the fingernails of an open hand viewed from above, grouped two two-airplane elements for flexibility and mutual support.

BELOW RIGHT
JAAF fighter flights in China initially flew in a three-airplane "V" formation left over from World War I. In combat, these formations were likely to break down into individual aircraft, leaving Japanese pilots vulnerable to unseen attackers. By 1944, Ki-43 units were beginning to adopt the much more flexible four-ship formation used by the USAAF and RAF in the CBI.

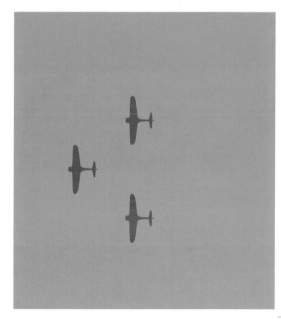

Sadly, a large proportion of JAAF pilots did in fact fight to the death during World War II, although Kuwahara, by a quirk of fate, was not one of them.

The differences in training techniques of the two air forces came into play when their fighter pilots encountered each other in combat, to be sure. But ultimately it was the sheer scope of the two nations' efforts to train pilots for combat that would set them apart.

From the beginning, Japanese war planners failed to understand this issue. When the Japanese Army established its Army Youth Pilot Program in 1938 to begin building up strength for the coming war, its initial intake was just 120 student pilots in two schools. By contrast, a year later when the United States started the Civilian Pilot Training Program, its first-year goal was to produce 20,000 new pilots. The numbers continued to be skewed as time passed.

By the end of the war, Japan had produced some 46,000 pilots, while no fewer than 193,440 Americans had earned their wings between 1941 and 1945. From December 1942 through to August 1945, the USAAF graduated 35,000 fighter pilots from its FRTUs alone.

Even when considering that the United States was fighting on two fronts while Japan was not, the sheer weight of numbers of American pilots made the outcome of the Pacific air war a foregone conclusion.

ORGANIZATION AND TACTICS

The operational units of the USAAF and JAAF were organized similarly. The numbered air forces of the USAAF corresponded to the JAAF's air armies, and both were assigned to specific geographical areas. In China, the USAAF's Fourteenth Air

P-40 pilots of 74th FS/23rd FG pose for a group photograph during the summer of 1944. They are, in the front row from left to right: unknown, Wallace Cousins and John Wheeler; in the second row, from left to right: unknown, Ted Adams and Jim Crawford; and in the top row, from left to right: Louis Anderson, Bob Martin, unknown, Robert Woodward, Charlie Cook and Fred Bear. (John Wheeler)

Force was headquartered in Kunming, while the JAAF's 5th Air Army headquarters was in Hankow.

The basic operational unit was the group in the USAAF and the hikosentai, usually shortened to "sentai," in the JAAF. A USAAF group normally consisted of three or four squadrons further broken down into several flights. On paper, a USAAF squadron would have about 25 aircraft and pilots, with the basic formation being four flights of four aircraft each. This was rarely the case in the Fourteenth Air Force, however, where a full squadron formation was extremely rare due to the paucity in aircraft and pilots. More likely, twelve, eight or even as few as four fighters would be involved in a mission.

In the JAAF, the equivalent of the squadron was the "chutai," of which there were usually three in a sentai. Each chutai normally comprised 16 aircraft and pilots, and it was further broken down into flights of three called "shotai," the smallest flying section. Later in the war, the three-airplane shotai gave way to the more effective four-airplane formation used by the Allies.

It was in the utilization of their fighter units that the American and Japanese commanders diverged. Gen Chennault, commander of the Fourteenth Air Force, had gained fame as the architect of the dive-and-zoom attacks on the agile Japanese fighters that his AVG pilots used so successfully during 1941–42. But an overlooked, and perhaps just as important, aspect of his tactics was the employment of P-40s in the fighter-bomber role.

Although the first P-40s in China were used primarily in pure fighter roles such as interception and bomber escort, by 1944 the majority of their missions involved attacking ground targets, including airfields, road and river traffic, railways, troop concentrations and army compounds in Japanese-held territory. The numbers of P-40s involved in these missions varied depending on the availability of aircraft, pilots, fuel and ammunition, but the standard configuration involved 12 aircraft in three flights of four.

The assault flight would make the first attack, with the remaining two flights providing top cover. Then the assault flight would climb up and replace one of the

Col Casey Vincent flies his P-40K "7" over Kunming Lake in early 1943. Credited with six victories prior to being restricted from combat flying by Gen Chennault, Vincent named this Warhawk *Peggy* after his wife. It is believed that the airplane had previously been assigned to Col Robert L. Scott while he was commander of 23rd FG. (Bruce Holloway)

CLINTON D. VINCENT

Born in the small town of Gail, Texas, on November 29, 1914, Clinton D. Vincent was the youngest of 11 children in his family. Known throughout his life by the nickname "Casey," Vincent moved with his family to Natchez, Mississippi, while still a small boy, and grew up there. On graduating from high school in 1932, he received an appointment to the prestigious United States Military Academy at West Point.

After graduating from West Point as a second lieutenant in June 1936, Vincent undertook flight training at Randolph and Kelly Fields at San Antonio, in Texas. His first operational assignment came in November of the following year when he became the operations officer for the 19th Pursuit Squadron at Wheeler Field, in Hawaii. A move to California followed in November 1940, when Vincent transferred to the newly formed 35th Pursuit Group. He advanced rapidly in the group from squadron commander to group operations officer, executive officer and, in December 1941, group commander with the rank of major.

Vincent left for Australia in January 1942 and eventually wound up in Karachi, India, in March. There, he was assigned as Director of Pursuit Training for the Tenth Air Force. This was effectively a desk job, and he loathed it. Finally, in November 1942, Vincent obtained a transfer to BrigGen Claire Chennault's staff in China. He flew his first two combat missions on November 11 while en route to Kunming, China, from Dinjan, India. Upon arrival in China, Vincent was named operations officer of the CATF. Flying with the 23rd FG, he received credit for his first aerial victory – a fixed-gear fighter shot down over Canton – on November 27, 1942.

Vincent was promoted to full colonel in January 1943 and became chief of staff of the Fourteenth Air Force when it was activated in March. At about this time he began to be depicted in the popular Milton Caniff comic strip *Terry and the Pirates* as "Colonel Vince Casey." Then, in May 1943, he assumed command of the Forward Echelon of the Fourteenth Air Force at Kweilin, while continuing to fly missions whenever time allowed. On August 26, 1943, he scored his sixth and last confirmed victory, after which Gen Chennault grounded him from further combat flying.

After spending September and October on leave in the US, Vincent was named commander of the newly created 68th Composite Wing (an expansion of the Forward Echelon) in December 1943. His promotion to brigadier general in June 1944 at the age of 29 made him the youngest American general since the Civil War. Vincent continued to command the 68th CW throughout the *Ichi-Go* offensive, and returned to the US in December 1944.

Fellow ace BrigGen David L. "Tex" Hill, who served as Vincent's deputy in the 68th CW, recalled "'Casey' was one of the greatest officers I've ever been around. He was strong, smart – just one hell of a good man. He was never recognized for what he did. He handled it well in China. But you could tell in his diary that he felt like he'd been left hanging."

Vincent served in Air Defense Command postwar and died of a heart attack in his sleep on July 5, 1955. He was just 40 years old.

TOSHIO SAKAGAWA

Toshio Sakagawa was born in 1910 in Awaji Shima, Hyogo Prefecture, and graduated from the Army Military Academy with the 43rd Intake in October 1931. Promoted to flying second lieutenant, he was sent to Tokorozawa for pilot training and then received instruction on fighters at Akeno. Following a posting to the 1st Rentai, Sakagawa enrolled in the commander's course and graduated in July 1936. His next posting was to the Type 91 parasol fighter-equipped 11th Rentai in Harbin, China, as commander of the 2nd Chutai.

Sakagawa's first combat experience came shortly after the outbreak of war with China in 1937, when his unit was forced to fly ground support missions in the northern regions of the country due to there being no aerial opposition of note in this area. Sent back to Japan in March 1939 to briefly serve as an instructor at Akeno, in Japan, he duly returned to China in September 1939 as commander of the Ki-27-equipped 3rd Chutai, 24th Sentai. His unit took part in the final attack on Tamsagbalu on the 15th of that month at the end of the Nomonhan Incident.

After his promotion to major in August 1941, Sakagawa assumed command of the 47th Independent Fighter Chutai, which was formed at Tachikawa from personnel previously assigned to the Flight Test Center and equipped with nine pre-production Ki-44s. Dubbed the "Shinsegumi" or "Kawasemi" unit, the 47th moved to Saigon on December 8, 1941 and operated over Malaya and Singapore until April 1942, when the unit was transferred back to Japan. Frustrated by the Ki-44's short range and poor serviceability, Sakagawa and his pilots had enjoyed little success in combat.

In October 1942 Sakagawa was posted to command the Ki-43-equipped 25th Sentai, which had just formed following the expansion of the Canton-based 10th Independent Fighter Chutai. He and his unit would enjoy considerable success through to July 1944, with the highlights for Sakagawa including the destruction of a B-24 Liberator over Hankow on August 21, 1943 – the first time a JAAF fighter had downed a four-engined USAAF heavy bomber in China. Sakagawa's biggest day in combat came on May 6, 1944, when he claimed the destruction of three P-51 Mustangs in a single combat over Hongchung. As CO of the 25th Sentai, he led the unit with great distinction during the opening stages of the *Ichi-Go* offensive.

In July 1944, Sakagawa transferred back to the Akeno school, and three months later he was named deputy commander of the oversized 200th Sentai. Equipped with Ki-84s, this unit boasted six chutais staffed with former instructors drawn from the Akeno school. Sakagawa fought with this unit in the Philippines in October and November, and was then sent to the Ki-84-equipped 22nd Sentai on December 1, 1944 as its new CO. After three more weeks in combat in the Philippines, and having lost more than 20 pilots, the 22nd was ordered back to Japan to recuperate. In a cruel twist of fate, on December 19, 1944, a transport airplane carrying surviving 22nd Sentai pilots home crashed during a night take-off from Fabrica airstrip, on the Philippine island of Negros. Sakagawa was among those passengers killed. Postwar historians believe he claimed about 15 victories in aerial combat.

Maj Toshio Sakagawa taxis out in his Ki-43-II "00" at Hankow on July 13, 1944, shortly before the ace was posted to Akeno, in Japan, to become deputy commander of the large 200th Sentai. Sakagawa, who claimed around 15 aerial victories, died in a flying accident on December 19, 1944. (Yasuho Izawa)

other flights in the top cover as the second flight of four aircraft went down to attack. Finally, the third flight would follow. If enemy aircraft approached to challenge the mission, the top cover would be ready to take them on while the low flights got out of harm's way.

The JAAF used its Ki-43s far more as pure fighters. This made sense, given the fact that the airplane, with its light armament, was designed specifically for air-to-air combat and not the bombing and strafing of ground targets. In China, Ki-43 units used two tactics to attempt to lure P-40 pilots into combat at a disadvantage. One was to send a single fighter down below a high-flying formation of Ki-43s to act as bait. If P-40s attempted to attack the lone Ki-43, the others would dive on the American adversaries from above.

A second tactic was one the American pilots soon dubbed the "squirrel cage." In this, a formation of Ki-43s would break into two Lufbery defensive circles, one above the other, traveling in opposite directions. Every so often, Ki-43 pilots would loop, roll and perform other maneuvers in their highly agile Oscars as they flew in their circle. From a distance, the "squirrel cage" looked like a big dogfight, but if a Warhawk pilot approached with the idea of joining the fight, he would quickly find himself surrounded by unfriendly Ki-43s. In practice, American pilots quickly became wary of these two ploys, and rarely took the bait.

COMBAT

On March 8, 1944, Col Winslow B. Morse, commander of the Fourteenth Air Force's CACW, was at his headquarters in Kweilin, China, when he received urgent orders to proceed at once with his staff to Kunming for a meeting with his commander, MajGen Chennault. Something big was in the wind. For two months, Chinese intelligence had been monitoring the Japanese movement of supplies and troops south from Peking and Manchuria via rail to the Yellow River Bridge, near Chenghsien. Chennault had concluded that the Japanese were building up for a push south across the river and through Honan Province in an attempt to complete the rail link with Hankow. In response, he devised a strategy to oppose the advance by air attack, which he called "Mission A," code name *Fateful*.

Units of Morse's CACW would provide most of the air power for "Mission A," including one B-25 squadron of the 1st Bomb Group (BG) and the four squadrons of the 3rd FG, equipped with P-40Ns, as well as two P-40 squadrons of the 4th FG CAF for support. Initially, this small force (a total of 84 aircraft on the rare days when all squadrons were at full strength) would operate from airfields at Liangshan, Hanchung, Ankang and Enshih.

The CACW was perhaps the least heralded and most misunderstood of all the Fourteenth Air Force units that fought in China during World War II. In action from November 1943 to the end of the war, the CACW rolled up an impressive record against the Japanese while overcoming the challenges of culture and language posed by having Chinese and American personnel serving side-by-side in its squadrons.

The CACW was born in May 1943 at the Trident Conference in Washington, D.C., when Chennault sold the conferees on a plan to build up Allied air strength in China. At that time, US-trained Chinese pilots were becoming available in substantial numbers, but the CAF was short on aircraft and leaders with combat experience.

The USAAF, on the other hand, was experiencing a shortage of new combat pilots, but had plenty of new airplanes being delivered from factory assembly lines.

Under Chennault's plan, the CACW would use a mirror command structure, with Chinese and American co-commanders from wing headquarters all the way down to flight leaders and administrative positions in the wing's eight fighter squadrons and four medium bomber units. Chinese personnel would fill out the remaining slots for flight crews and technicians. The CACW would be a unit of the CAF, and its aircraft would carry Chinese markings. But unlike other CAF units, it would serve under the operational control of Chennault and the Fourteenth Air Force.

Operational training of the first three CACW squadrons commenced in August 1943 at Malir Cantonment, near Karachi, India (now Pakistan). The desert air base would be the birthplace of all CACW squadrons, which would number 12 by the time the last ones had completed training nearly a year later. The CACW itself was officially formed at Malir on October 1, 1943, under the command of Col Morse and his Chinese counterpart, Col Chiang I-Fu. Initially, the wing consisted of the 3rd FG (Provisional), with P-40Ns, and the 1st BG (Provisional), flying B-25Ds. The 5th FG (Provisional) was formed in January 1944, also flying P-40Ns. Eventually, each group consisted of four squadrons.

The 28th and 32nd FSs flew the CACW's first fighter missions on December 1, 1943, a week after they had arrived at Kweilin and set up operations. By the following spring, all four P-40 squadrons of the 3rd FG (7th, 8th, 28th and 32nd FSs) and two squadrons of the 5th FG (its last two squadrons were soon to arrive) were operating in China alongside USAAF P-40 units of the 23rd FG.

The plan behind "Mission A" was to let the Japanese concentrate their Honan forces, then smash them with air attacks before the offensive had time to begin. Air raids would continue to be flown until the Japanese withdrew. At air bases around Hankow, the 5th Air Army of the JAAF had four fighter sentais (totaling roughly 100 aircraft) available to support the advance. The veteran 25th Sentai, equipped with

Ki-43-IIs, had been operating in China since late 1942. Another Ki-43 unit, the 48th Sentai, was newly arrived from Manchuria, while the 9th and 85th sentais had begun receiving Ki-43s to bolster their shrinking complements of Ki-44s.

Col Morse made a flying tour of his new bases following the meeting with Chennault, then settled down to make plans for "Mission A" while awaiting the "go" order from Fourteenth Air Force headquarters. But the carefully laid plans involving notification by the Chinese four weeks prior to the peak of the build-up were quickly discarded when Japanese troops crossed the Yellow River in force on April 19, 1944 – with no warning from the Chinese! As Japanese tanks and cavalry rolled south from Chenghsien, it was obvious that the opportunity to stop the offensive before it started had been lost. To make matters worse, bad weather descended on eastern China, forcing Morse's squadrons to delay departure for their new bases for a critical week.

By May 1, three P-40 squadrons had reached Liangshan and were ready for action, but again the weather turned nasty and the airplanes went nowhere for three more

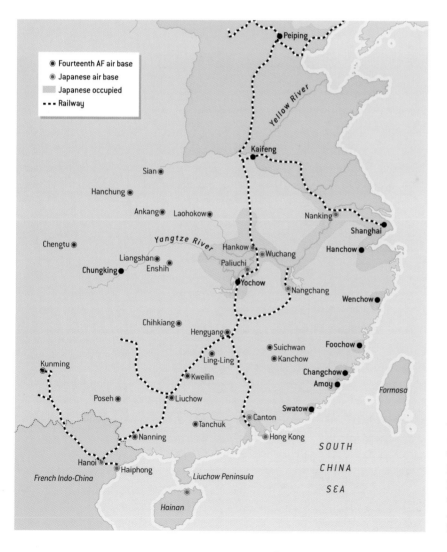

From its air bases in China, the USAAF's Fourteenth Air Force could strike targets in the Japanese-held areas of Hankow, Canton/Hong Kong, French Indo-China and Burma, as well as harassing Japanese shipping lanes in the South China Sea.

days. Meanwhile, the Japanese were pushing southward in several drives, with little substantive opposition from Chinese ground forces. The 32nd FS, meanwhile, had reached its base at Hanchung and flew its first of many strikes against the Yellow River Bridge on May 3, dive-bombing the storage area on the north side of the single-track, two-mile-long span. Heavily defended and easy to repair, the bridge would be hit repeatedly in the coming months, but it was never closed for more than a few days.

On May 5, the 32nd FS registered the first claims for aerial victories of "Mission A." Led by squadron commander, Maj William L. Turner, eight P-40s were strafing a section of the Luchow-Loyang road (which would quickly be nicknamed "Slaughterhouse Alley") when Turner and Capt Keith Lindell spotted a single-engined aircraft they identified as a "Val" (probably a JAAF Mitsubishi Ki-51 ground attack aircraft) and teamed up to shoot it down. Capt Tom Maloney and LtCol Tom Summers (3rd FG fighter control officer, assigned to fly with the 32nd FS) destroyed a twin-engined transport airplane that they encountered nearby a short while later.

The P-40s continued their strafing mission, and Summers' aircraft was struck by ground fire, forcing him to bail out. He returned to Hanchung on foot some days later. Lt Wang was wounded when an explosive shell hit his P-40 in the cockpit, and he crash-landed near Loyang. The P-40s' strafing proved effective, destroying 40 to 50 trucks, four armored cars and two pillboxes, plus killing an estimated 200 Japanese soldiers.

By this time, the full scope of the *Ichi-Go* offensive was becoming clear to the Americans. Col "Casey" Vincent, CO of the 68th CW at Kweilin, put together a force of 54 fighters and bombers for a strike against the Hankow area on May 6 in the hope of destroying Japanese supplies before the second phase of *Ichi-Go* could begin its drive down the Hsiang River valley toward Changsha. Led by Col David L. "Tex" Hill (legendary AVG ace now serving as commander of the 23rd FG), the fighter force consisted of P-51s of the 76th FS, P-38s of the 449th FS and P-40s of the 75th FS.

The formation pressed northeast toward Hankow through heavy haze and scattered clouds. About ten minutes out from the target – a supply area just off the edge of the main Hankow airdrome – several Ki-43s popped out of the clouds and made a head-on pass at a flight of Mustangs, and one P-51 was shot down. Soon the P-38s and P-40s joined the scrap, but only Col Hill, flying a P-51, would claim a victory. 1Lt James Folmar of the 75th FS was also credited with damaging a Ki-43. The Oscars were unable to engage the bombers, which successfully attacked the target.

At this point, the fight was on for aerial supremacy in the skies over the *Ichi-Go* advance. Although distracted by the CACW's aggressive attacks in Honan Province, the JAAF 5th Air Army took on as its main assignment the securing of air superiority over the Hengyang and Suichwan areas, where the 68th CW bases were located. On May 11 and 12, the Japanese sent out strong missions against Suichwan, which was located in a pocket of Chinese-held territory midway between Hankow and Canton.

The first attack on the Suichwan area arrived in the late afternoon of the 11th when 35 Ki-43s of the 25th Sentai were reported heading toward the auxiliary air base at nearby Namyung. A small 76th FS force of three P-40Ns and two P-51Bs scrambled to meet the attack, with Capt Ed Collis leading. The P-40s attacked a "V" formation of Ki-43s from behind, and the Japanese pilots dropped their wing tanks when they saw the P-40s closing in. Collis, nevertheless, was able to get a good burst into the tail of one of the Hayabusas, which went down trailing smoke, and the Warhawk pilot later spotted a fire on the ground where he believed the airplane had crashed. Collis was credited with a confirmed victory, and the other three members of his flight each got one damaged. Lt Bill Watt described the fight:

We in the P-40s sighted about 12 "Oscars" flying 1,000ft below us. We dove down and succeeded in each one of us killing an "Oscar". As I remember, there wasn't much to it. I just picked off one of the "Oscars" and got the hell out of there. We made it back to Suichwan without being intercepted by the Jap aeroplanes flying top cover.

The CACW was also in action on May 11, with P-40 pilots of the 7th and 32nd FSs claiming six Ki-43s shot down for no losses during a scrap near Mienchih.

The pilot and groundcrew assigned to this 1st Chutai/85th Sentai Ki-44 strike a proud pose in front of their aircraft in China. The pilot appears to be Capt Akira Horiguchi, who commanded the chutai from June through December 1943. (Hiroshi Ichimura)

The Japanese *Ichi-Go* Offensive, which would provide the impetus for the last major confrontation involving the P-40 and the Ki-43, eventually deprived the USAAF's Fourteenth Air Force of all of its major air bases in eastern China.

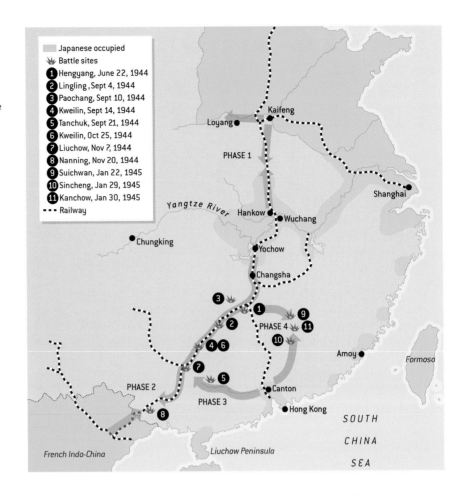

Japanese occupied
Battle sites
1 Hengyang, June 22, 1944
2 Lingling, Sept 4, 1944
3 Paochang, Sept 10, 1944
4 Kweilin, Sept 14, 1944
5 Tanchuk, Sept 21, 1944
6 Kweilin, Oct 25, 1944
7 Liuchow, Nov 7, 1944
8 Nanning, Nov 20, 1944
9 Suichwan, Jan 22, 1945
10 Sincheng, Jan 29, 1945
11 Kanchow, Jan 30, 1945
- - - Railway

The results of these opening encounters of the P-40-versus-Ki-43 *Ichi-Go* duel cannot be confirmed on the Japanese side, but the advantage seems to have gone to the American fighters. The JAAF evened the score the following day when the 5th Air Army sent more missions to the Suichwan/Namyung area.

For the first mission on May 12, the JAAF despatched nine Ki-48 bombers of the 90th Sentai, escorted by about 50 Ki-43s of the 25th and 48th sentais. The Chinese warning net failed yet again, and the Japanese force reached Suichwan without being intercepted at about 0630hrs. Three P-40s and three P-51As of the 76th FS, along with P-40Ns of the 29th FS/5th FG CACW, scrambled late and were still climbing when the Japanese formation arrived over the base. The bombers flew past the airfield, turned around and made their bombing runs heading north in the direction of home. One flight of Ki-43s made a strafing run across the field as well.

Lt Steve Bonner, leading the P-40s of the 76th, dived toward the base and made a head-on pass at one of the Hayabusa strafers, seeing strikes on its engine as the two airplanes passed. Then he attacked another Ki-43 from above and behind, getting hits on the wing root and forward fuselage. The fighter went down trailing heavy smoke and fire, and ground observers confirmed its crash. This victory made Bonner an ace with five kills, all scored in P-40s.

Fellow P-40 pilot Lt Ken Elston of the 29th FS claimed a Ki-43 destroyed for the 5th FG's first confirmed victory of the war, and two P-51 pilots were also credited with victories. The Japanese lost two Ki-43s and their pilots, Sgts Katsuji Kurosaka and Souki Hoshi, from the 48th Sentai, and claimed one P-40 and one P-51 shot down. The only US loss was the P-40 of Lt Irving Saunders of the 76th FS, which belly-landed at its base, caught fire and burned – Saunders escaped injury. Another P-40 pilot, Lt Bob Kruidenier of the 29th FS, gave this account of the mission, which confirmed the stoutness of the P-40 airframe:

The gun camera of Col Bruce K. Holloway's P-40 catches a shot of a Ki-43 crossing into very dangerous territory in front of the American fighter's six 0.50-in. machine guns. "I was pretty close," Holloway noted on the back of the original photo print. (Bruce Holloway)

I fired at plenty of Jap fighters that day, and while I was squaring away for a sure kill, a Nip let me have it with all he had. Holes appeared in the canopy, and oil and smoke filled the cockpit. In a flash I knew I had let myself become a "sitting duck" for some Jap pilot. I rolled the aeroplane over on its back and headed for Mother Earth, knowing that my would-be killer would not follow me down in a high dive, as the Jap aeroplanes were not capable of withstanding terrifically high diving speeds. I found that my wheels and flaps would still function, and I was able to make a safe landing on our own field. Not until I viewed the holes in my aeroplane did I realize what a lucky boy I had been. Except for five small needle-like steel splinters which had entered my right leg, I was still all in one piece.

The Japanese came back in the afternoon in another big formation, but this time only a few P-51s and P-40s were available to defend the base. The Japanese lost two Ki-48s, but their bombing was very effective. One string of bombs fell directly across the revetment area, destroying three P-38s and damaging three B-25s and three P-40s. After this, the 5th Air Army shifted its attention to the air bases at Hengyang, Lingling and Kweilin, also staging occasional night raids against the CACW at Liangshan.

On May 17 the 25th Sentai sent 27 Ki-43s to attack the American air base at Hengyang, hoping to cripple the 23rd FG by catching its fighters there on the ground. The plan did not work, however, as most of the P-40s were returning from a mission at the time and were diverted to Lingling for landing. Two pilots from the 75th FS, Lts Oswin "Moose" Elker and Vernon Tanner, were assigned to airfield defense. They took off when the Japanese fighters were reported, and climbed to the bottom of an overcast layer at 4,000ft. Elker gave this account of what happened next:

As the Ki-43s reached the field, they got into what we called their "squirrel cage" formation, in which some circled in one direction and some in the opposite direction. Some looped and some rolled. The purpose of this tactic was to give them good visibility in all directions against attack from any angle. More than anything else, it resembled a bee swarm.

As they came below us, Tanner and I attacked those that came within our range. The attacked Japs always headed into the "squirrel cage" where, due to the diverse maneuvers of their comrades, there would always be one of them to attack the pursuer. I made short attacks and got back into the overcast to lose my pursuers, of which there were always several. After a quick turn in the overcast I'd come back down, and with so many aeroplanes in such a small patch of sky, there was a good chance I would sometimes come back down behind one within range. I would usually get in one good burst before I'd have tracers coming over my shoulder and I would have to get back into the overcast.

Elker got in a good burst at a Hayabusa on one pass and saw it spiral down trailing smoke, before breaking back into the clouds. He turned in the claim as probably destroyed, along with four damaged. Tanner also claimed a probable, but was badly hit himself and had to belly-land his P-40 at Hengyang. Several other 75th FS pilots managed to tackle the "squirrel cage" late in the fight, and total claims by the squadron were one confirmed destroyed, four probables and six damaged. The 25th Sentai claimed two P-40s shot down in exchange for two Ki-43s lost (with pilots Lt Koji Morita and Cpl Fukuji Tagami), plus three more damaged.

Elsewhere on May 17, Japanese troops in Honan Province completed their operation to link the Peking-Hankow railway line. With that, the "Mission A" units shifted their emphasis to denying the Japanese use of the line and began raining down bombs, rockets and machine-gun fire on trains and bridges from dawn until dusk. Then, on May 26, the main phase of the *Ichi-Go* campaign began when the Japanese 11th Army crossed the Yangtze River near Yochow and headed south toward the river city of Changsha. Chinese resistance was light at first, but it stiffened as the invaders crept closer to the city, where Gen Hsueh Yueh was in command of nearly 150,000 defenders.

Immediately, the pace and profile of 68th CW operations changed. Now, in addition to striking at Japanese installations and defending their own airfields, pilots would also begin attacking Japanese troop concentrations and lines of communication in the field. The flying took a toll, as the 75th FS alone lost seven

Capt Keisaku Motohashi, in Ki-43-II "80," leads two more Hayabusas of the 25th Sentai out for a mission from Hankow in 1944. "62" was piloted by Cpl Hruyuki Toda, while 2Lt Iwataro Hazawa was at the controls of "51." (Yasuho Izawa)

P-40s (two pilots killed) between May 26 and 29, including two aircraft destroyed by Japanese bombs at Hengyang.

The JAAF's 5th Air Army stepped up its activities as well in an effort to lend support to the ground advance. The 25th and 48th sentais began flying their Ki-43s from Paliuchi, just above Tungting Lake, which was the closest base to the Hsiang Valley fighting from which they could operate safely without the constant threat of air attack. The Hsiang Valley advance moved swiftly and was soon out of range of the short-legged Ki-44s of the 9th Sentai at Hankow, the 85th Sentai's Ki-44s having moved south to Canton in preparation for a new drive that would soon start north from there.

Ki-43s were also based at Linfen to support the fighting in Honan Province, but several of these aircraft were destroyed on May 31 by rocket-firing P-40s of the 32nd FS/3rd FG.

Flying was curtailed by rain on this front during the first week of June. Then on the 9th, Chinese ground forces began a limited drive toward the city of I-ch'ang, west of Hankow. This drive was supported by CACW P-40 squadrons at Enshih and Liangshan, the 8th and 28th FSs reporting a lively scrap with Ki-43s over I-ch'ang on that date. But the Chinese soon stalled short of their objective, and the advance was called off by month-end.

June was busier for the American and Japanese pilots fighting over the Hsiang River Valley as the land offensive rolled on. Col Vincent moved 5th FG squadrons and the 76th FS from Suichwan to Hengyang on June 1 to bolster the defenses there. Two days later, the 76th sent its P-51s to Lingling, while the 74th FS brought its P-40s to

Two P-40Ns of the 75th FS/ 23rd FG sit on alert in front of the operations shack at Hengyang in the spring of 1944. "188" was the regular mount of Capt Don Glover, and the victory flags denoting his two confirmed kills are visible below the windscreen of his airplane. The regular pilot of "186" *PISTOL PACKIN' MAMA* is not known. (Everett Hyatt)

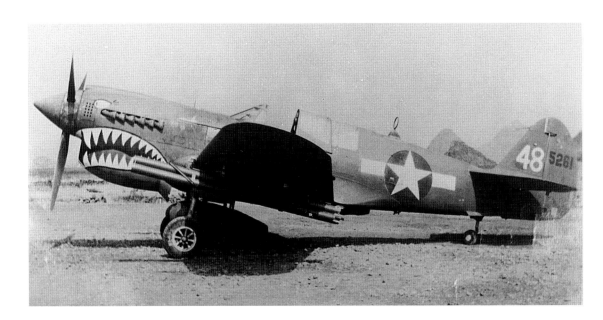

P-40N "48" (42-105261) of the 74th FS/23rd FG has been fitted with rocket tubes under its wings prior to flying a ground attack mission from Kweilin. The regular pilot of this aircraft was Capt Thomas P. Bennett, who registered his last combat claim – a Ki-43 probably destroyed near Changsha – on June 11, 1944. (Luther Kissick)

Hengyang from Kweilin. On June 9, the 5th FG moved to a new base at Chihkiang, 175 miles northeast of Hengyang, where it would operate for the next year.

A new P-40 squadron joined the 23rd FG mid-month when the 118th Tactical Reconnaissance Squadron (TRS) arrived at Kweilin under the command of future ace Maj Edward McComas.

The 23rd FG flew nine missions on June 9 alone, including five by the 74th FS. Two days later the depleted 75th FS pulled back to Kweilin. Now only the 74th FS remained at Hengyang, but this would not last for long.

On June 15, Japanese ground forces bypassed Changsha, effectively accomplishing their first goal for *Ichi-Go* by bottling up the Chinese troops there, and continued heading south. This placed the air base at Hengyang, only some 80 miles away, in jeopardy. For more than two years Hengyang had been the "hot corner" in eastern China due to its close proximity to the Japanese strongholds at Hankow and Canton. Whenever Fourteenth Air Force fighter pilots got orders sending them to Hengyang, they could feel pretty confident of seeing plenty of action. Now those days were ending.

On June 16 Col Vincent ordered the 74th FS (down to eight P-40s, with just three of them fit for combat) to pull back to Kweilin. When the Japanese reached the gates of the city four days later, the last US personnel were ordered to evacuate the air base, and Vincent then had it demolished that night. By morning, nothing remained of the base that had been the scene of so many of the 23rd FG's greatest triumphs bar smoking rubble and a runway pock-marked with bomb craters.

But the Chinese 10th Army chose to make a stand at Hengyang, although the city was now surrounded. Some 10,000 troops, commanded by Gen Fong Hsien Chien, held the Japanese at bay, despite being equipped with just three old 75mm cannon and a smattering of machine guns, mortars and rifles. The siege at Hengyang would stretch on for the next six weeks, while the Japanese also continued to advance down the Hsiang Valley.

The primary gunsight in the P-40N was the USAAF's N-3A reflector sight, manufactured by Service Tool Engineering of Dayton, Ohio. The N-3A, like reflector sights used by other combatant air forces during World War II, was essentially a refined ring-and-bead, with the image of the ring-and-bead projected by a light onto a special glass in front of the pilot's eyes so that they were only visible when the pilot was looking directly down the longitudinal axis of his aircraft.

The most important improvement that the N-3A offered over the ring-and-bead sight was that the reflector's image was focused at infinity, so the pilot did not face the impossible task of trying to focus his sight on two different distances — the sight and the target — at the same time.

The brightness of the image could be adjusted to suit the light conditions. The graticule could also be adjusted to the wingspan of the target aircraft, so when the latter's wingspan filled the circle, the pilot knew he was in range. The graticule was also of some help to the pilot in calculating deflection while firing at a target turning away from him, but it was basically no more helpful than a ring-and-bead sight in this regard.

P-40s were also fitted with a ring-and-bead sight as a manual back-up in case the reflector sight failed.

The USAAF subsequently introduced the more sophisticated K-14 gyroscopic gunsight in 1944, but few if any of these were fitted to late-production P-40N Warhawks.

Lousy weather during the first three weeks of June – the peak of the monsoon season – did not prevent the P-40s from severely pounding the advancing Japanese forces. The majority of the missions flown were river sweeps designed to catch the Japanese hauling men and supplies by boat south to their frontline troops. In one nine-day period, the 23rd FG flew 538 sorties and lost just one aircraft when the engine failed in the P-40N flown by Lt David Rust of the 75th FS. He was forced to make a wheels-up landing ten miles north of Lingling.

For the month of June, the 23rd FG flew 1,606 offensive sorties – more than double the number flown in May, piling up 3,790 hours of combat time in the process, and claiming 17 Japanese aircraft shot down. But the price was high, with 20 P-40s and 12 P-51s lost to all causes. Few of these losses were attributed to enemy fighters, however, because the bad weather severely hampered operations of the Ki-43s from Paliuchi.

The first big engagement of the month took place on June 25, when Maj Arthur Cruikshank led a mixed formation of 74th and 75th FS P-40s out of Lingling on an offensive sweep up the river north of Hengyang. At mid-morning, the P-40s encountered eight Ki-43s of the 25th Sentai that were escorting Ki-51 ground attack aircraft sent to attack the Chinese at Hengyang. The Ki-51s turned for home as the P-40s and Ki-43s clashed. One of the American pilots on the mission was Lt Robert S. Peterson of the 75th FS, who was flying as wingman for Lt James C. Vurgaropolus. Peterson recalled fighting two enemies that day – Japanese fighters and the weather:

Lt Robert S. Peterson of the 75th FS/23rd FG was able to register an air combat claim from his first encounter with enemy aircraft, probably destroying a Ki-43 of the 25th Sentai over the Hsiang River Valley on June 25, 1944. Peterson scored two confirmed victories during his combat tour in China, and went on to retire from the USAF Reserve with the rank of major general. (Bob Peterson)

I was glued to Vurgaropolus, this being my first contact with Jap fighters. We dove on a fighter (Ki-43), and when Vurgaropolus scored hits on him, he turned across my sight and I got in a good burst. As we were outnumbered, we dove away without seeing the aeroplane hit the ground. We claimed a probable, sharing half each.

While this action was going on, the weather had moved in between us and Lingling. We had become separated from the others, so "Vurgie" told me to form up on his right wing and we would follow the Hsiang River back to Lingling. He took the left bank and I took the right. The river twisted and turned between high banks. It was typical monsoon rain. The rain was so heavy I could hardly see "Vurgie's" aeroplane – water was coming in around the canopy. At that moment the aeroplane shuddered and I saw wire draped over and around the nose and canopy. I had run through telephone lines that crossed the river. On landing, the wire was strung out 1,200ft behind me.

The P-40 pilots claimed three Japanese fighters destroyed, five probables and four damaged for the mission, while their opponents claimed one P-40 damaged. Neither side reported any losses that day. Peterson went on to complete 94 missions in China and eventually retired from the USAF Reserve as a major general. Vurgaropolus was not so lucky. He was killed just four days after the June 25 mission when his P-40 slammed into a building during a strafing run over Changsha.

As June drew toward its close, the air base at Lingling was the next to be threatened by the Japanese advance. By this time, the crucial air raid warning net was breaking down in the Tungting Lake area, leaving the base exposed to air attack as well. The 75th FS moved to Kweilin and the 76th went farther south to Liuchow, where its Mustangs would be in position to oppose a new Japanese advance moving northwest out of Canton.

July brought further scraps between Japanese and American fighters. The JAAF's 5th Air Army had instructed its bomber and fighter pilots to concentrate on attacking ground targets – Chinese defensive positions and supply lines – and to avoid air combat whenever possible. But considering the intense air operations over the rather narrow area of the *Ichi-Go* advance, such encounters were inevitable.

Capt Takashi Tsuchiya (1st Chutai/25th Sentai leader) scored eight victories before he was killed in action on September 3, 1944. The label on his parachute harness read *Chutai-cho* (Chutai leader). His Ki-43-II was marked as aircraft "20." (Yasuho Izawa)

On the morning of July 5, the 75th FS sent eight P-40s, led by Maj Donald L. Quigley, from Kweilin to escort B-25s attacking a supply depot at Tungcheng, some 40 miles east of Tungting Lake. The weather cleared as they passed Lingling, and just north of Hengyang Lt Donald Lopez spotted 12 Ki-43s of the 25th Sentai coming in from above. Quigley advised the bombers to clear the area as he led the P-40s in a sharp turn to meet the Ki-43s head-on. He fired on a Ki-43 as it passed below him and saw the airplane stagger as it was hit. Quigley rolled over on his back and watched the Ki-43 dive straight down. By this time both formations had broken up, and aircraft were spread all over the sky. Quigley attacked another Ki-43 from the rear and saw it erupt in flames before he was forced to break off his attack.

Lopez, leading the second flight of four P-40s, picked up some battle damage in the opening pass and lost his wingman, Lt Al Haines, who was shot down to become a POW. Then Lopez took a long-range shot at a Ki-43 below him. The maneuverable Hayabusa immediately stood on its wingtip and clawed into a hard turn to port – a maneuver that the P-40 pilots called a "flip" – and Lopez lost it. Next he saw a Ki-43 below him turning to the right and gave chase. Following its turn, Lopez pulled so much lead that the target dropped out of sight behind the long nose of his P-40. He opened fire with a short burst, eased off the turn enough to observe the results, then

pulled hard again and fired a longer burst. This time when he eased out of his turn, he could see the Ki-43 trailing fire from its engine cowling and wing roots as it fell away.

The second element in Lopez's flight was also involved. Lt Joshua Sanford and his wingman, Lt Art Heine, shot up two Ki-43s that were attacking Lopez during the opening pass. Sanford picked out another target and was hitting it when yet another Oscar got on his tail and put a solid burst into the P-40's fuselage and cockpit area. Sanford was wounded in the foot and broke off into a dive. He was able to fly homeward as far as Lingling, where he belly-landed the damaged Warhawk.

In an obvious case of misidentification, the 25th Sentai pilots claimed two P-51s shot down and two damaged against no losses. The P-40 pilots were credited with three confirmed victories for the loss of the P-40s flown by Haines and Sanford. Three more encounters took place later in the day, with the 25th Sentai losing Cpl Shoji Kanayama near Sinshih, shot down by Lt Harold Robbins of the 74th FS.

Another significant air battle that gives excellent insight into the intensity of the operations took place on July 15, when P-40s of the 74th FS ran into a formation of 48th Sentai Ki-43s – and possibly Ki-44s (referred to in the following account as "Tojos") of the 9th Sentai – during a mission to Siangtan. What follows is the post-mission narrative obtained from the flight leaders of the 74th FS:

The 74th FS sent seven P-40s led by Capt John C. Herbst, squadron commander, from Kweilin to stage out of Namyung against the Japanese supply line from Tungchang to Tsyungyang. On July 14 they attacked several truck columns and destroyed more than 50 vehicles. Early the next morning they staged out of Suichwan to attack barracks and flak positions near Siangtan. The dive-bombing flight, led by Capt Theodore A. Adams, carried a 250lb bomb under each wing. The trio of top cover, led by Capt Herbst, was loaded with parafrags (parachute fragmentation bombs).

The flights approached Siangtan, with the top cover at 8,000ft and the dive-bombers at 6,000ft. Capt Adams was to lead two dive-bombers in on the barracks near the airfield and Lt Virgil A. Butler and his wingman were to attack flak positions near the railway trestle north of the city.

Capt Theodore Adams supplied the following account of his experiences during the mission:

I had just located the target and peeled off on my dive-bombing run when I noticed a silver aeroplane below and to the right of me. It had a high, square-tipped wing and a radial engine. I kept an eye on the silver job because I figured I would come back after I bombed and get it. When I got down to about 2,000ft I saw another Jap to my left. I dropped my bombs and went after him. He was turning across my nose, so I pulled in behind him. I had built up so much speed in my dive that I closed in a hurry.

Lts Don Lopez (left) and Dick Jones of the 75th FS/23rd FG look over the damaged left aileron of the former's P-40N shortly after returning from a mission on July 5, 1944. Lopez was credited with one Ki-43 destroyed and one damaged during the fight that had taken place that day near Hengyang. These two pilots had joined the 75th FS as replacements in November 1943, and both men registered their first aerial victories less than a month later. (Don Lopez)

I started shooting with a 30-degree deflection and closed so fast I had to duck under to keep from hitting the Jap. He was a "Tojo" with elliptical wings and a big radial engine. I saw smoke trail out of his engine and then he fell off and hit the ground. I was at about 1,200ft when I pulled out.

I saw a whole mass of Japs milling around the field at about 1,000ft. There were at least 20 "Tojos" and "Oscars" in a big landing circle going clockwise around the field. I did a steep 180-degree turn and came back over the field. I blacked out in the turn and headed into the Jap circle. One "Tojo" started to pull straight up away from the circle. I still had plenty of excess speed so I followed him up in a vertical climb. We were both going straight up when I opened fire. I saw two big plumes of black smoke trail from his cowling, and he stalled out. I had to duck again to avoid a collision. I saw him go down smoking like a chimney.

There was a "squirrel cage" formation south of the field, with eight "Oscars" chasing their tails and edging away from the main fight. My speed was still up, so I broke into the edge of their circle. One tried to dive out so I gave him a 30-degree burst. I missed, and all of a sudden there were four other "Oscars" coming in on me from behind. They were shooting, but their deflection was off – all trailing. I dived a little and another P-40 came scooting by and scattered the Japs.

I came back over the field at 500ft and saw a "Tojo" going west. I overhauled him and took a 45-degree deflection shot and then cut it down to 20 degrees. I saw pieces fly off his fuselage, but he kept on going. By this time one of my coolant lines had cracked and the fluid was boiling out. My temperature gauge was clear over on the peg, so I shoved the nose down and started for the Chinese side of the lines to the southwest. Two Japs chased me, and I could see four others on the tail of another P-40. The Japs couldn't gain on me, and the coolant saw me home. I found out later that Lt Van Sickle had shot an "Oscar" off my tail as I turned into my first "Tojo." I never even knew the Jap was there.

Lt Virgil Butler also spoke about his experiences on July 14:

I was after some flak positions near the railway trestle north of the field. I made my bomb run and went after the silver square-winged Jap. All of a sudden I picked up three Japs on my tail. While I was diving and twisting to get away from them, a "Tojo" loomed up ahead in my sights. He had his flaps and wheels down, and was almost dead ahead below me. I lowered my nose and took a good long shot from squarely astern. He looked as though someone had struck a match along his fuselage – just a long, growing flare of flame. He rolled over and crashed, still burning. I kept on diving down to the deck and got away from the other three Japs.

Finally, Capt John Herbst gave his take on how the mission went from his point of view:

I was leading the top cover at 8,000ft when I heard Capt Adams call, "There is a Jap down here". At the same time I spotted three black fighters coming in toward us. They

A groundcrewman inspects the nose of P-40N "49" of the 74th FS/23rd FG, which was forced to make a belly landing at Kweilin after receiving damage in a scrap with JAAF fighters. Judging from the hit in the left flap area, the airplane suffered a failure of its hydraulic system. (Leon Klesman)

must have been top cover for whatever was going on below. I turned into them and they turned away. I never did see them again. We dropped our frag bombs and belly tanks and started down. We picked up a terrific speed in that dive – enough to carry us all the way through the fight with an advantage.

At 3,000ft I saw two black columns rising from two Jap aeroplanes that had already hit the deck. Then I spotted a lot of Japs at about 1,000ft circling clockwise, and a couple of P-40s weaving in and out of the circle. There were two dust streamers rising along the runway where two more Japs were taking off. I counted at least 16 "Oscars" and "Tojos" all strung out in the circle, apparently following their leader. They made no effort to get away – just went around and around.

I started to cut inside the circle, but I had so much speed – about 340mph – that I had to weave in and out to get shots in. It was a real slugging match. We had the speed and altitude on them, and at close range those six 0.50s tore them apart. I took a couple of snapshots and missed. The Japs just went round and round – none of their usual tricks, not even steep, tight turns. They seemed to be afraid to do any stunts at low altitude. Our boys had been flying on the deck for so long – strafing and dodging hills in bad weather – that nobody thought twice about racking around in vertical banks ten feet off the deck. It was just our "meat."

I spotted an "Oscar" with his wheels down at about 600ft. I slowed down and came in directly behind him and a little above. I gave him a two-second burst and he erupted in flames. I saw him crash. By then I had picked up a "Tojo" on my tail, with an "Oscar" behind him. I could also see other smoke columns rising from crashed aeroplanes. The "Tojo" opened fire, but all his shots were trailing. I could out-turn him, but the moment I got ahead the "Oscar" would cut across the circle and cut me off. I flipped over and started turning in the opposite direction. The same thing happened. I was surprised that I could turn inside the "Tojo", but he seemed unwilling to make a tight turn at 500ft. Finally I shoved the stick down and dived under the "Oscar" as he banked across to cut me off. That cleared my tail, and I looked around.

There was a P-40 south of the field with a "Tojo" on his tail at 800ft. The P-40 was diving and the "Tojo" turning into him to get a deflection shot ahead of him. I turned into the "Tojo" from high astern. My first burst was over him, and he saw the tracers. He flipped over and tried to dive out in the opposite direction. That brought him squarely into my sights for a no-deflection shot, and I gave him another burst that nearly burned out my guns. He burned and went in. I got back up to 500ft and came back across the field. There were only three Zeros left still circling the field. I went after them, along with about five other P-40s. We made a couple of passes and didn't hit anything. Leaving the field, I saw columns of smoke rising from the ground.

The Ki-43 pilots claimed one P-40 destroyed, one probable and two damaged, although in fact there were no Warhawk losses. The P-40 pilots claimed six victories, including two Ki-43s and four Ki-44s. The 48th Sentai did indeed lose two Ki-43s, with Capt Tadashi Nishikawa and SgtMaj Susumu Ito both being killed.

July also saw the 5th FG at Chihkiang fly three very effective missions against the JAAF airfield at Paliuchi. These strikes, flown on the 14th, 24th and 28th, are probably the best-remembered missions in the history of the group. The combined score was 66 Japanese aircraft destroyed, 31 probables and 24 damaged, for the loss of one P-40 and its pilot to enemy action and one other to a flying accident.

Aggressive low-level flying and superb planning can be credited for the success of the Paliuchi missions. Each time, the P-40s approached the target by flying across Tungting Lake at wave-top height, and each time they caught the Japanese by surprise. A measure of just how unprepared the enemy was for these attacks is revealed in one simple statistic – of the 66 aircraft destroyed, only two were shot down. The rest were caught on the ground, helpless before the guns and bombs of the P-40s.

While these aerial battles were taking place, on the ground, the Chinese defenders continued to hold out in Hengyang thanks to supplies dropped to them from

Although faster than the earlier models of the Hayabusa, the Ki-43-III was already obsolete by the time it debuted in 1944. Here, China-based American soldiers inspect a captured Ki-43-III fitted with droppable wing tanks. (Craig Busby)

Fourteenth Air Force transport airplanes. Yet despite aircraft from Col Vincent's 68th CW mercilessly pounding Japanese ground troops surrounding the city, and "Mission A" units continuing to disrupt the enemy's lines of supply, Hengyang was doomed. The air action climaxed on August 8, 1944, the very day the Chinese finally capitulated after a siege lasting 44 days.

That morning, P-40Ns of the 75th FS/23rd FG had an encounter with Ki-43-IIs of the 48th Sentai at low altitude near Hengshan. The 23rd FG mission recap read as follows:

Eight P-40s of the 75th took off from Lingling at 0450hrs for an offensive sweep and patrol from Hengyang north to Siangtan, following the river. Four barges and one powered sampan damaged. Nine trucks burned and 18 damaged. After this the "Sharks" (P-40s) ran into nine "Oscars" and "Hamps" (in actuality, all Japanese fighters involved were Ki-43s). Lt (Robert) Peterson confirmed one "Hamp." Maj (Donald) Quigley got one probable "Oscar". Lt (James) Folmar probably destroyed one "Oscar." Lt (Donald) Lopez damaged one "Oscar." Lt (Joseph) Martinez damaged one "Oscar" and Lt (Paul) Moehring damaged two "Oscars." All of our aeroplanes returned safely.

The 75th FS's mission description read in part, "Maj Quigley found an 'Oscar' apparently crippled and chased it all the way to Lukow on the deck. He got in three head-on passes, and several times the aeroplane seemed to be out of control, but always recovered right on the deck. Maj Quigley ran out of ammunition and broke away without seeing the aeroplane go in." Lt Robert Peterson recalled years later "a fight down to the treetops. This was a situation we had long been warned against –

Members of the 3rd FG/CACW pose with performers from a USO entertainment troupe in front of the P-40N flown by Lt Col William N. Reed at Liangshan in August 1944. The performers, in the center of the photograph, were Ruth Dennis, actress Ann Sheridan, Mary Landis and comedian Ben Blue. Reed is at far left, partially blocked from view by Col T. Alan Bennett, commander of the 3rd FG. (John Hamre)

Ki-43-II "55" of the 25th Sentai at Nanking. Note that the fighter's tail number does not match the number on the landing gear cover. The mottled camouflage was field-applied, thus no two Ki-43s in the 25th Sentai looked alike. (Yasuho Izawa)

dogfighting with Jap Zeroes – but I got into the fight and refused to let go until my foe went down."

The Ki-43 pilots of the 48th Sentai claimed no fewer than seven P-40s shot down, although in fact none were lost. Three Ki-43s were destroyed and their pilots killed, and Sentai commander Maj Masao Matsuo was badly injured in a fourth machine.

Also on August 8, LtCol Bill Reed, the former AVG pilot now serving as commander of the 7th FS/3rd FG, led 11 P-40s of the 7th, 8th and 28th FSs off from Enshih at 1300hrs, heading east to sweep the Yangtze River to Hankow. The P-40s approached the target area at 3,000ft in CAVU (ceiling and visibility unlimited) weather, then descended to treetop level at Sinti and strafed several concentrations of boats spotted along the river. While at low-level, the P-40s were jumped by more than 12 Ki-43s of the 25th Sentai. The 7th FS mission report described the fight as follows:

> They proceeded toward Hankow, where they were jumped by enemy fighters. LtCol Reed got on the tail of one "Oscar" after it had pulled off a pass on a P-40 and gave it a good burst. Lt (Edward) Mulholland (Reed's wingman) saw him in an uncontrolled glide at less than 500ft. Claimed one destroyed. Lt Mulholland got a 40-degree deflection shot at an "Oscar" and gave him three good bursts. It flipped on its back with flames coming from its engine in a steady stream. Claimed one destroyed. Lt Mulholland got hits on two other "Oscars" in head-on passes. Claimed two damaged. Lt Tang became lost on the return trip and landed at Kaifeng.

The P-40 pilots claimed a total of nine Ki-43s destroyed, but the encounter was not actually that decisive. The 25th Sentai lost one Ki-43 in the fight and claimed three P-40s shot down. In fact, no P-40s were lost, although LtCol Reed came home with a big hole in the right aileron of his airplane.

The capture of Hengyang was another victory for the Japanese, but it had come at a high cost. The *Ichi-Go* ground forces, now extended like a finger into Hsiang River Valley, were fatigued, and their supply line was tenuous at best because of its continued vulnerability to air attack. Similarly, the 5th Air Army was nearing exhaustion. The 25th Sentai was down to just a handful of Ki-43s and the 48th Sentai was in even worse shape. After having lost 16 pilots and most of its Ki-43s over the previous three months, the 48th was withdrawn to re-equip with new aircraft and replenish its pilot strength. Within a few weeks the 22nd Sentai would arrive from Japan, equipped with the new Nakajima Ki-84 Hayate – a far superior fighter to the Ki-43.

The P-40 units opposing the Japanese remained full of fight, but their ability to maintain pressure on the Japanese was compromised by shortages of fuel and ammunition. And the number of P-40s in frontline service was beginning to wane as high-performance North American P-51 Mustangs displaced them in squadron after squadron.

The war in China would continue for another year, but the full-scale aerial duels between P-40s and Ki-43s were now all but over.

2Lt Iwataro Hazawa (front row center) was one of the most successful pilots in the 25th Sentai, with an estimated 40 claims for aircraft destroyed or damaged before he was killed in action on January 14, 1945 at Hankow. Another ace in the picture, Sgt Maj Kyushiro Ohtake (upper right), survived the war. (Yasuho Izawa)

STATISTICS AND ANALYSIS

The air battles involving P-40s and Ki-43s over China during the summer of 1944 constituted a classic confrontation between two contemporary fighter aircraft and the pilots who flew them. The airplanes were dissimilar in design and performance, while the pilots were products of two distinctly different cultures. But in the final analysis, the difference in the war-making capabilities of the United States and Japan was the deciding factor in the outcome of the fight.

On the American side, Gen Chennault's fighter pilots achieved the immediate goal of maintaining control of the air over the various fronts in the *Ichi-Go* advance. Fourteenth Air Force interdiction missions continued unabated throughout the campaign, hindered more by bad weather than by occasional interceptions by Japanese fighters. In fact, a P-40 pilot was far more likely to be shot down by Japanese ground fire than in air-to-air combat. For example, the 23rd FG lost 20 P-40s and 12 P-51s in June 1944 to all causes, but only one loss was the result of being shot down by an enemy fighter. The group lost 24 more fighters in July and 30 in August, eight of which went down in air-to-air combat.

The ability of the Fourteenth Air Force to absorb such losses without losing control of the skies was due in part to the aggressive nature of its combat leaders, and in part to the fact that its units received sufficient replacement aircraft and pilots.

In contrast, the JAAF's 5th Air Army sustained heavy losses in air-to-air combat and from enemy raids on its airfields. The Japanese started the *Ichi-Go* campaign with 113 Ki-43s and Ki-44s – roughly equal to the number of Fourteenth Air Force fighters opposing them – but the numbers of airplanes and pilots in the 5th Air Army quickly declined as replacements failed to cover losses.

Very early in the campaign, Japanese commanders could already see their forces being depleted, so they ordered their pilots to avoid air combat whenever possible. But this proved impractical because the JAAF fighter units were tasked with defending the Japanese supply lines, which were constantly under attack from American fighters and bombers. As the supply lines grew longer, so Japanese losses mounted. Pilot strength in the 25th Sentai, for example, had dropped from 44 on May 31 to just 25 by the end of August.

But the fact remains that Gen Chennault could not stop the Japanese ground advances by hitting them from the air, as he had confidently predicted he would be able to do prior to the offensive commencing. The Chinese army simply lacked the skills and equipment to hold its ground, despite all the help it got from the Fourteenth Air Force.

Perhaps the most telling statistic lies in the production numbers. The Ki-43 was the most numerous JAAF fighter of World War II, a grand total of 5,751 being delivered in just over four years. By comparison, the P-40's production run of 13,738 aircraft ranked just third among USAAF fighters behind two superior types, the P-47 and the P-51. Even if the Ki-43 had possessed superior combat capabilities, which it definitely did not, the Oscar still would have fought a losing battle due to the inability of Japan, and its aircraft manufacturers, to keep pace with their counterparts in the United States.

This group of 1st Chutai/25th Sentai pilots included three aces. They are, front row, from left to right, 2Lt Iwataro Hazawa (15 victories), Capt Hiroshi Kusano (1st Chutai leader from September 1944 to the end of the war), WO Tadao Tashiro (eight victories) and MSgt Kyushiro Ohtake (10+ victories). The two men standing in the back row are unidentified. (Yasuho Izawa)

ACES LISTS

Several factors make it difficult, bordering on impossible, to produce a definitive statistical analysis of the P-40 vs Ki-43 duel in China. For one thing, American pilots tended to identify all Japanese radial-engine monoplane fighters as "Zeros," even after the existence of the JAAF's Ki-43s and Ki-44s became known in 1943. The Fourteenth Air Force maintained a policy of requiring verification from a second source to confirm aerial victories, but the nature of air warfare still made confirmation an inexact art at best.

P-40 ACES IN CHINA WITH FOUR OR MORE Ki-43 KILLS				
Name	Unit	Ki-43 kills	Total score	Notes
Maj E. W. Richardson	23rd FG	7	8-0-0	75th FS CO
Maj A. W. Cruikshank Jr	23rd FG	6	8-6-0	74th FS CO
Capt J. F. Hampshire Jr	23rd FG	6	13-3-0	KIA China, 2/5/43
Col B. K. Holloway	23rd FG	6	13-4-0	23rd FG CO
Capt J. W. Little	23rd FG	6	7-0-0	1 kill Korea
Maj R. L. Callaway	3rd FG CACW	5.5	6-1-2	32nd FS CO
Capt D. A. Clinger	23rd FG	5	5-3-0	–
Maj E. R. Goss	23rd FG	5	6-2-0	75th FS CO
LtCol R. L. Liles	23rd/51st FGs	5	5-5-2	16th FS CO
Capt J. M. Williams	23rd FG	5	6-2-1	76th FS CO
Capt H. A. Paxton Jr	3rd FG CACW	4.5	6.5-0-2	–

TOP Ki-43 ACES WHO SCORED IN CHINA 1942–45			
Name	Sentai	Total score	Notes
Capt I. Hosono	25th	26	KIA China, 6/10/43
1Lt M. Kanai	25th	26	19 victories over China
Capt N. Ozaki	25th	25	KIA China, 27/12/43
WO M. Ogura	24th	16	1st P-40 victory July 1942 China
LtCol T. Sakagawa	25th	15+	KIFA Negros, Philippines, 19/12/44
SgtMaj T. Shono	25th	14	KIA China, 27/10/44
Maj K. Namai	33rd	12	1 P-40 victory China
2Lt I. Hazawa	25th	10+	KIA China, 14/1/45
SgtMaj K. Ohtake	25th	10+	–
WO E. Seino	25th	10+	4 P-40 victories China
SgtMaj K. Kato	11th	9	3 P-40 victories early 1944 China
WO T. Tashiro	25th	8	KIA China, 4/1/45
Capt T. Tsuchiya	25th	8	KIA China, 3/9/44
SgtMaj M. Yamato	33rd	8	3 P-40 victories August 1943 China
Capt H. Shishimoto	11th	7	–

The JAAF put far more emphasis on the overall group performance in combat, preferring to give credit for aerial victories to the unit rather than to an individual pilot. In addition, the JAAF established no specific rules for confirming the veracity of a victory claim. Thus, the tallies listed here are based on the victory claims attributed to the pilots at the time of this publication being written.

Finally, due to the shortage of detailed Japanese records from the China campaign, it is impossible to break down all JAAF aces' scores by enemy aircraft type. Most of the tallies attributed to the leading Japanese aces in China would almost certainly have contained at least one P-40 kill, however, as the Warhawk was the only American fighter in-theater for much of World War II.

Capt Raymond L. Callaway of the 8th FS/3rd FG/CACW poses in the cockpit of his P-40N "681" (fuselage code "03") in August 1944. He claimed his third and fourth of six eventual victories on August 8, 1944 – the day the Hengyang siege ended – and he later commanded the 32nd FS/3rd FG. (Ray Callaway)

AFTERMATH

The *Ichi-Go* offensive continued after the fall of Hengyang, as did aerial clashes involving P-40s and Ki-43s. But bad weather in September and October 1944, combined with the declining number of P-40s in China, made these encounters increasingly rare.

By this time, the Fourteenth Air Force was finally getting high-performance North American P-51B/C Mustangs as replacements for its tired P-40s, as Gen Chennault had been requesting for two years. All former P-40 squadrons of the 23rd and 51st FGs had been re-equipped with Mustangs by the end of 1944, and the CACW squadrons would follow suit in the spring of 1945. Meanwhile, the 5th Air Army continued to fly Hayabusas, its Ki-43-IIs slowly giving way to the new Ki-43-III model, along with Ki-44s and the vastly superior, but notoriously unreliable, Ki-84 Hayate.

On January 14, 1945, CAF Lt Yueh Kung-Cheng of the 27th FS/5th FG CACW was credited with shooting down a Ki-43 during an escort mission to Hankow, thus giving him the distinction of claiming what is likely to have been the last P-40 victory over a Hayabusa in China, if not the entire Pacific War.

But the Japanese ground offensive in China wore on. Kweilin and Liuchow had fallen in November 1944, followed by Suichwan and Kanchow in January 1945. These conquests completed the *Ichi-Go* objective of establishing a rail link from Indo-China to Shanghai and Peking, but it was a hollow victory because the continuing ability of the Fourteenth Air Force to strike the railway line from its remaining bases made the link all but useless.

Seeking to put a stop to this aerial harassment, the Japanese next turned their attention to the Fourteenth Air Force's forward airfield at Chihkiang, where the 5th FG CACW and the 75th FS/23rd FG were based. An offensive by the 20th Army began in the spring of 1945, with limited aerial support from the JAAF's diminished 5th Air Army. This time, however, the Chinese defenses held and the Japanese drive stalled short of its goal in May 1945. P-40s and Ki-43s played little or no part in this final battle of the *Ichi-Go* offensive.

The P-40 went out of frontline service in the Fourteenth Air Force when the CACW's 27th FS/5th FG converted to P-51s in June 1945. P-47 Thunderbolts had already replaced Warhawks in the fighter-bomber role in Burma and the MTO in 1944, and former P-40 squadrons in the Pacific were now flying P-38 Lightnings. Most air forces retired their remaining P-40s at the end of the war. The Netherlands East Indies Air Force flew the last known combat operations in the P-40, attacking Indonesian nationalist guerillas on occasion before leaving the country in 1949.

Back in the US, the Curtiss-Wright Corporation was struggling while the rest of the nation was looking forward to the end of the war. As noted earlier, attempts to design a follow-on fighter to replace the P-40 on Curtiss production lines had proven to be unsuccessful.

The final version of the Warhawk, the XP-40Q, was a big improvement over the P-40N, but was still too little, too late. Upgrades included a cut-down rear fuselage spine and a bubble canopy, radiators moved to the wing roots to allow a more streamlined nose and a more powerful Allison engine with two-stage supercharging that produced a top speed of 422mph at 20,000ft. This would have been great had North American's superior P-51D not already been in full production. The P-40Q simply was not needed, and the last Warhawk rolled out of the Curtiss factory in November 1944. Plagued by chronic mismanagement and

The first Mustangs to reach China were these Allison-powered P-51As, which were assigned to the 76th FS/23rd FG in the autumn of 1943. They were hand-me-downs from the 311th FG in India, and they served alongside P-40s in the 76th until the following spring when improved P-51Bs began to arrive. (Bob Colbert)

a series of uninspired designs, the Curtiss-Wright Corporation eventually ceased all aircraft production in 1951.

The Ki-43 remained in production throughout the war. In fact, Tachikawa was testing a new model for home defense – the Ki-43-IIIb with heavier armament and a more powerful engine – when the armistice was signed. Few new Hayabusas reached China in the final year of the war, however, as virtually all fighters built in Japan were now being sent to units protecting the home islands, which were coming under attack from USAAF B-29 Superfortresses based in the Marianas Islands. By mid-November 1944, the 25th Sentai at Paliuchi had been reduced in strength to just nine Ki-43s and three Ki-84s.

In late January 1945, the 5th Air Army was ordered to prepare for an expected invasion on the east coast of China by pulling its units back to a triangular zone marked by the cities of Shanghai, Hanchow and Nanking. In its place, the smaller 13th Air Division was established at Hankow to carry on the fight in central China. After replenishment in Japan following the Hengyang siege, the 48th Sentai remained in China with its Ki-43s through to the end of the war. The 25th Sentai was ordered to Korea in June to prepare for the invasion of Japan, and it was still there when the war ended in September 1945.

The Oscar continued to serve in several Asian air forces until the late 1940s. As a member of the Greater East Asia Co-Prosperity Sphere, Thailand had received Ki-43-IIs from Japan in 1944, and its air force flew them in frontline service for several years after the armistice until they were replaced by more modern American and British types. In contrast, the Red Army of China forces acquired Ki-43s from former Japanese bases when they occupied Manchuria beginning in October 1945. Similarly, insurgents of the Indonesian People's Security Force built up their air force by refurbishing a number of wrecked Hayabusas that had been recovered from a large aircraft dump in Djakarta.

Although appearing at first glance to be intact, derelict Ki-43 "71" is missing its left aileron and tailwheel assembly as it sits forlornly on an airfield at Nanking in September 1945. Dumped Oscars littered ex-JAAF airfields across the Pacific and China-Burma-India Theater at war's end. (Yasuho Izawa)

The French confiscated Ki-43s from the JAAF's 64th Sentai at the end of the war and used them for a short period on counter-insurgency operations in French Indo-China until replacing them with Spitfires acquired from the British. The French pilots initially had difficulty landing their Oscars, being unfamiliar with them, and several were wrecked. This was said to have amused the demobilized Japanese pilots still in the country, because they considered the Ki-43 very easy to handle both in the air and on the ground.

Ironically, the postwar era was kinder to Nakajima Aircraft than it was to Curtiss-Wright. At the end of the war, after producing a total of 25,935 airplanes and 46,726 aircraft engines over the previous 30 years, Nakajima was broken up into 15 smaller companies. These firms began making products utilizing aviation technologies, such as monocoque buses, scooters that rolled on bomber tail wheels and other transport-related products.

Later, five of these companies reunited into what is currently known as Fuji Heavy Industries Ltd, a manufacturer of transportation- and aerospace-related products, as well as the maker of Subaru vehicles. So, 60 years after the end of World War II, the legacy of the Nakajima Ki-43 Hayabusa is a popular car found on American highways from coast-to-coast!

These Ki-43s, Ki-44s and Ki-84s were also found parked on the airfield at Nanking at the end of the war. The two closest Ki-84s are in the markings of the 9th Sentai, and appear to be in reasonably good operational condition. (Bill Bonneaux)

FURTHER READING

Books

Band, William F. X., *Warriors Who Ride The Wind* (Castle Books, 1993)

Bueschel, Richard M., *Nakajima Ki-27A-B* (Arco Publishing, 1970)

Bueschel, Richard M., *Nakajima Ki-43 Hayabusa I-III* (Arco Publishing, 1970)

Byrd, Martha, *Chennault giving Wings to the Tiger* (University of Alabama Press, 1987)

Christy, Joe and Jeff Ethell, *P-40 Warhawks At War* (Charles Scribner's Sons, 1980)

Francillon, René J., *Japanese Aircraft of the Pacific War* (Putnam, 1970)

Green, William and Gordon Swanborough, *Japanese Army Fighters, Part Two* (Arco Publishing, 1978)

Hata, Ikuhiko, Izawa, Yasuho and Christopher Shores, *Japanese Army Air Force Fighter Units and their Aces 1931–1945* (Grub Street, 2002)

Heiferman, Ron, *Flying Tigers – Chennault in China* (Ballantine Books Inc, 1971)

Johnsen, Frederick A., *P-40 Warhawk* (MBI Publishing, 1998)

Kawahara, Yasuo and Gordon T. Allred, *Kamikaze* (Ballantine Books, 1957)

Kissick, Luther C., *Guerrilla One* (Sunflower University Press, 1983)

Lopez, Donald S., *Into the Teeth of the Tiger* (Bantam Books Inc, 1986)

McClure, Glenn E., *Fire and Fall Back* (Barnes Press, 1975)

McDowell, Ernest R., *Curtiss P-40 in Action* (Squadron/Signal Publications, 1976)

Molesworth, Carl and H. Stephens Moseley, *Wing To Wing* (Orion Books, 1990)

Molesworth, Carl, *Sharks Over China* (Brassey's, 1994)

Molesworth, Carl, *Osprey Aircraft of the Aces 35 – P-40 Warhawk Aces of the CBI* (Osprey Publishing, 2000)

Pentland, Geoff, *The P-40 Kittyhawk In Service* (Kookaburra Technical Publications Pty Ltd, 1974)

Rosholt, Malcolm, *Days of the Ching Pao* (Rosholt House, 1978)

Rosholt, Malcolm, *Flight in the China Air Space, 1910–1950* (Rosholt House, 1984)

Sakaida, Henry, *Osprey Aircraft of the Aces 13 – Japanese Army Air Force Aces 1937–45* (Osprey Publishing, 1997)

Shores, Christopher, *Curtiss Kittyhawk Mk I–IV in RAF, SAAF, RAAF, RNZAF, RCAF, NEIAF Service* (Osprey Publications Limited, 1971)

Snyder, Louis L., *The War, A Concise History 1939–1945* (Simon and Schuster, 1960)

Taylor, John W. R., *Combat Aircraft of the World* (Putnam, 1969)

Wagner, Ray, *American Combat Planes* (Doubleday & Company, 1968)

Windrow, Martin C. and René J. Francillon, *The Nakajima Ki 43 Hayabusa* (Profile Publications, 1969)

Magazines

Yasuo, Izawa, "Combat Dairy of the 64th Sentai – The Red Eagles Part Two," *Air Classics* (Vol. 8 No. 10): pp.38–45

Molesworth, Carl, 'From Mustang Driver to Museum Director', *Air Classics* (Vol. 16 No. 2) pp.46–53

Molesworth, Carl and H. Stephens Moseley, "Fighter Operations of the Chinese-American Composite Wing," *American Aviation Historical Society Journal* (Vol. 27 No. 4) pp.242–257

Rabena, Oscar H., "Japanese Air Power In The Second World War – Its Strengths and Weaknesses," *OSS Digest* (Volume 4.3)

Web Sites

http://www.76fsa.org
http://www.airwarfareforum.com
http://www.americanfighteraces.org
http://www.armyairforces.com
http://www.cbi-history.com
http://cbi-theater.home.comcast.net/menu/cbi_home.html
http://cbi-theater-5.home.comcast.net/roundup/roundup.html
http://www.flyingtiger.org
http://www.flyingtigersavg.com
http://forum.axishistory.com
http://genemcguire.com
http://hawksnest.1hwy.com/In%20Service/InService.html
http://www.j-aircraft.com
http://www.p40warhawk.com
http://www.sinoam.com
http://surfcity.kund.dalnet.se/sino-japanese-1942.htm
http://205.188.238.109/time/magazine/article/0,9171,803293,00.html
http://www.aviation-history.com/nakajima/ki43.html

INDEX

References to illustrations are shown in **bold**.